W9-AJT-942

Better Homes and Gardens®

Summertime Grilling

Summertime Grilling

Pictured on the cover: Grilled Burgers Italiano (see recipe, *page 41*)

Project Editor: Lois White

Project Designer: Nancy Wiles

Contributing Writer: Anne Ytzen Colville

Contributing Copy Editor: Winifred Moranville

Test Kitchen Director: Sharon Stilwell

Production Manager: Ivan McDonald

Vice President, Publishing Director: John Loughlin

Publisher: Mike Peterson

Editor In Chief: Don Johnson

Senior Project Editor: James D. Blume

Design Director: Jann Williams

All of us at Meredith Corporation are dedicated to providing you with the information and ideas you need to create tasty foods. We welcome your comments and suggestions. Write to us at: *Summertime Grilling,* Meredith Custom Publishing, 1912 Grand Ave., Des Moines, IA 50309-3379.

It's summer, and one of America's greatest culinary traditions is on: the move outdoors for the enticing aroma and delicious taste of barbecue. Whether it's a picnic at the park, a neighborhood potluck, or a casual gathering in our own backyard, it seems many of our summertime activities center on a smoking grill. And now more than ever, we're expanding beyond our familiar barbecue standbys and discovering that just about everything under the sun tastes great cooked over the coals.

In this book, we've covered the bases for successful summertime grilling. Included is a foolproof guide for setting up and firing up your barbecue grill. You'll find more than 60 fabulous recipes, all tested and tasted in the *Better Homes and Gardens*® Test Kitchen. The recipes include tried-and-true favorites, from smoky ribs to sizzling steaks, plus nontraditional fare reflecting your desire for lighter tastes and ethnic flavors. You'll find a potpourri of flavoring strategies—marinades, spice rubs, and sophisticated salsas—all designed to enhance that intriguing charcoal-grilled taste we love. And, we haven't forgotten some tempting salads, dazzling desserts, and other exciting extras to complement your cookouts, plus menu suggestions throughout to help you bring all the terrific flavors of summer together for great warm-weather entertaining.

So grab your aprons, tongs, and skewers. We hope you'll be inspired by *Summertime Grilling*—now, and all year long.

Summertime Grilling

Grilled Chicken Salad
with Plum Vinaigrette
(see recipe, page 25)

*Rosemary-Marinated Swordfish
(see recipe, page 65)*

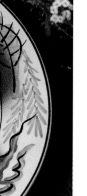

*Herb-Rubbed Steaks
(see recipe, page 30)*

Today's Cooking Made Easy

Backyard Entertaining

When the weather turns warm, Sharon Stilwell, *Better Homes and Gardens*® Test Kitchen director, enjoys entertaining family and friends in her own backyard. Here, she shares a favorite Southwestern barbecue, which includes make-ahead dishes and easy-to-grill recipes, leaving plenty of time to enjoy the great outdoors.

Pictured clockwise *from top:*

Fresh Fruit with Cherry Cream,
Double Apricot Margaritas,
New Potatoes with Roasted Garlic,
Grilled Pork Loin with
Southwestern Pesto Sauce,
Summer Slaw, and fresh vegetable crudités
with Creamy Salsa Dip.

(For recipes, check index, *page 96.*)

Entertaining with Ease

Take these shortcut cues from Sharon for getting maximum mileage from your grill.

The grilled roast is ready for carving in the kitchen.

• Plan as many make-ahead dishes as possible—a chilled fruit or pasta salad, for example. Marinate meat ahead of time, and prepare sauces or salsas early in the day.

• Consider indirect cooking. The food is turned less frequently, and there are fewer flare-ups, leaving the cook with more time for mingling.

• Grill poultry and roasts with the skin or fat on, then trim and serve. This keeps the food moist during cooking.

• Choose boneless roasts for easier and faster carving. Give one of your guests the honor of carving, while you arrange and garnish the serving platter.

• Wrap an herb-buttered loaf of bread in foil and heat on the grill.

• Heat vegetable casseroles—even baked beans—on the grill, using the indirect method. For easy cleanup, use disposable foil pans.

• Precook baking potatoes in your microwave oven. To give them a crispy skin like an oven-baked potato, reheat them alongside the grilled entrée.

• After a grilled meal, offer a simple dessert of lusciously ripe summer fruit.

CREAMY SALSA DIP

For a quick dip, stir together ½ cup *plain yogurt*, ½ cup *salsa*, and ⅓ cup *mayonnaise* or *salad dressing*. Cover and chill until serving time. Garnish with finely chopped *jalapeño pepper,* if desired. Makes about 1¼ cups.

GRILLED PORK LOIN WITH SOUTHWESTERN PESTO SAUCE

PREPARATION TIME: 10 MINUTES • MARINATING TIME: 4 TO 24 HOURS • GRILLING TIME:
1 TO 1¼ HOURS

½	teaspoon finely shredded lime peel
¼	cup lime juice
1	tablespoon cooking oil
2	cloves garlic, minced
1	tablespoon snipped fresh cilantro
1	teaspoon coarsely ground black pepper
¼	teaspoon salt
1	2-pound boneless pork top loin roast (single loin)
	Southwestern Pesto Sauce (see recipe, *below*)

◆ **For marinade,** combine lime peel, lime juice, oil, garlic, cilantro, pepper, and salt. Place pork roast in a plastic bag set into a deep bowl. Pour marinade over meat in bag. Seal bag; turn to coat well. Marinate in the refrigerator for 4 hours or overnight, turning occasionally.

◆ **Remove** meat from bag; reserve marinade.

◆ **In a covered grill** arrange *medium* coals around a drip pan. Test for *medium-slow* heat above the pan. Place roast on rack over drip pan but not over the coals. Cover and grill for 1 to 1¼ hours or until meat thermometer registers 160° to 170°, brushing occasionally with the reserved marinade. Serve with Southwestern Pesto Sauce. Serves 6.

◆ **Southwestern Pesto Sauce:** Cut 2 ounces *Mexican grating cheese* or *Parmesan cheese* (at room temperature) into pieces. Place the cheese; 1 clove *garlic,* peeled; and 1 small *jalapeño pepper* (see tip, *page 59*), seeded and cut into quarters in a blender or food processor bowl. Cover; blend or process until finely grated. Add one 4-ounce can *diced green chili peppers,* drained; ⅓ cup *pine nuts* or *slivered almonds;* 2 tablespoons lightly packed fresh *parsley;* and 2 tablespoons lightly packed fresh *cilantro leaves.* With machine running slowly, gradually add 1 tablespoon *olive oil.* Blend until nearly smooth.

NUTRITION FACTS PER SERVING WITH 2⅔ TABLESPOONS PESTO SAUCE: 348 cal., 40 g pro., 4 g carbo., 21 g fat, 98 mg chol., 1 g dietary fiber, 460 mg sodium.

DOUBLE APRICOT MARGARITAS

Relax on the deck with this icy double-fruit refresher.

PREPARATION TIME: 20 MINUTES

1¼ cups fresh halved, pitted, unpeeled apricots
       or one 16-ounce can unpeeled apricot
       halves (juice pack), drained
½ cup tequila
¼ cup sugar
¼ cup lime juice
¼ cup apricot nectar
20 to 24 ice cubes (about 3 cups)
       Lime juice
       Coarse salt

◆ **Combine** apricot halves, tequila, sugar, the ¼ cup lime juice, and the apricot nectar in a blender container. Cover and blend until smooth.

◆ **With the blender running,** add the ice cubes, a few at a time, through the hole in the lid, blending until slushy.

◆ **Rub** the rims of 8 to 10 glasses with lime juice. Invert glasses into a shallow dish of coarse salt. Shake off any excess salt. Pour in the margarita mixture. Makes 8 to 10 (4-ounce) servings.

NUTRITION FACTS PER SERVING: 81 cal., 1 g pro., 13 g carbo., 0 g fat, 0 mg chol., 1 g dietary fiber, 3 mg sodium.

DOUBLE APRICOT COOLERS (NONALCOHOLIC)

◆ **Prepare** margaritas as directed, *except* increase the apricot nectar to one 6-ounce can and omit the tequila.

NUTRITION FACTS PER SERVING: 56 cal., 1 g pro., 14 g carbo., 0 g fat, 0 mg chol., 1 g dietary fiber, 3 mg sodium.

Sharon's Flavoring Tips

Using her own backyard for inspiration, Sharon gathers a harvest of ideas for enhancing the flavor of grilled foods.

• Sharon collects loose bark and even small twigs from a backyard hickory tree, which, she says, "add distinctive smoke flavor to salmon, chicken, pork—you name it." Many times the wood is soaked first, but when time is short, the hickory is just thrown on the hot fire for instant smoke flavor.

• Pots of fresh herbs on Sharon's deck come indoors in the fall for year-round snipping. Fresh basil also grows in the garden, and after a heavy frost, Sharon saves the woody stems for throwing on the coals.

• For a super-quick idea, Sharon snips fresh sage leaves to place over chicken or fish during grilling.

• Sharon uses garlic chives for a speedy garnish, which she either ties in bundles to garnish platters or plates, or finely chops and sprinkles over vegetables or potato dishes.

Sharon chooses a rainbow of colorful vegetables to serve with the salsa dip.

FRESH FRUIT WITH CHERRY CREAM

PREPARATION TIME: 20 MINUTES • CHILLING TIME: UP TO 2 HOURS

  ½ cup whipping cream
  ¼ cup vanilla yogurt
  1 tablespoon sugar
  1 tablespoon kirsch or cherry liqueur, or orange juice
  4 cups mixed fresh fruit, such as sliced nectarines or peaches, whole raspberries, halved and pitted sweet cherries, and/or blueberries

◆ **Combine** whipping cream, yogurt, sugar, and liqueur in a chilled mixing bowl. Beat with chilled beaters of an electric mixer on medium speed until soft peaks form. Cover; chill for up to 2 hours. Dollop over fruit and serve immediately. Serves 4 to 6.

NUTRITION FACTS PER SERVING: 230 cal., 3 g pro., 29 g carbo.,12 g fat, 41 mg chol., 4 g dietary fiber, 0 mg sodium.

Barbecued Chicken
with Sesame-Chili Sauce
(see recipe, *page 14*)

Poultry

For summertime grilling,
poultry is the perfect
blank canvas to color with
your favorite ethnic and
regional flavors—from the
fiery-hot Caribbean accents in
the Jamaican Jerk Chicken to
the subtle Far-Eastern taste of
Turkey with Ginger Salsa.
Whether marinated, smoked,
or glazed, the succulent
chicken and turkey
entrées showcased here
become hot-off-the-grill
masterpieces.

BARBECUED CHICKEN WITH SESAME-CHILI SAUCE

Grill this sweet-spicy chicken for finger-lickin' raves! Pictured on pages 12–13.

PREPARATION TIME: 20 MINUTES • GRILLING TIME: 35 TO 45 MINUTES

⅔	cup plum sauce or sweet-and-sour sauce
¼	cup hoisin sauce
2	tablespoons soy sauce
2	tablespoons honey
2	tablespoons water
1½	teaspoons sesame seed
1	clove garlic, minced
1	teaspoon grated gingerroot or ¼ teaspoon ground ginger
¾	teaspoon Oriental chili sauce or several dashes bottled hot pepper sauce
¼	teaspoon five-spice powder
1	2½- to 3-pound broiler-fryer chicken, quartered or cut up

◆ **For sauce,** combine all ingredients *except* chicken in a saucepan. Cook over medium heat until bubbly, stirring often. Reduce heat. Cover and simmer for 5 minutes; set aside.

◆ **Remove** skin from chicken, if desired. Rinse chicken; pat dry. If using quartered chicken, break wing, hip, and drumstick joints so the pieces will lie flat during cooking. Twist wing tips under backs.

◆ **Place chicken,** meaty side down, on the rack of an uncovered grill directly over *medium* coals. Grill for 20 minutes. Turn; grill for 15 to 25 minutes more or until chicken is tender and no longer pink. Brush with sauce frequently during the last 10 minutes of grilling.

◆ **Transfer** chicken to a serving platter. Heat any remaining sauce either on the grill or stove top; pass with chicken. Makes 4 servings.

◆ **Make-ahead tip:** The sesame-chili sauce can be made up to 5 days ahead and stored, covered, in the refrigerator.

NUTRITION FACTS PER SERVING (SKIN ON): 417 cal., 33 g pro., 32 g carbo., 17 g fat, 100 mg chol., 0 g dietary fiber, 841 mg sodium.

GREAT GRILLING

Turn to the "Guide for Grilling Success" on pages 92–95 for hot tips on grills, tools, building and lighting the fire, and judging temperature of the coals.

Jamaican Jerk Chicken

"Jerked" chicken is traditionally marinated several hours in chili peppers and seasonings before being grilled. A dry seasoning rub is the shortcut method to this spicy dish.

PREPARATION TIME: 15 MINUTES • GRILLING TIME: 50 TO 60 MINUTES

2	teaspoons sugar
1½	teaspoons onion powder
1½	teaspoons dried thyme, crushed
1	teaspoon ground allspice
1	teaspoon ground black pepper
½ to 1	teaspoon ground red pepper
½	teaspoon salt
¼	teaspoon ground nutmeg
⅛	teaspoon ground cloves
1	2½- to 3-pound broiler-fryer chicken, quartered or cut up

◆ **For rub,** combine all ingredients *except* chicken in a small bowl.

◆ **Remove** skin from chicken, if desired. Rinse chicken; pat dry. If using quartered chicken, break wing, hip, and drumstick joints so the pieces will lie flat during cooking. Twist wing tips under backs. Sprinkle rub mixture evenly over chicken; rub in with your fingers.

◆ **In a covered grill** arrange *medium-hot* coals around a drip pan. Test for *medium* heat above the pan. Place chicken, bone side down, on the grill rack over the drip pan but not over the coals. Cover and grill for 50 to 60 minutes or until chicken is tender and no longer pink. Makes 4 servings.

NUTRITION FACTS PER SERVING (SKIN ON): 287 cal., 31 g pro., 4 g carbo., 16 g fat, 100 mg chol., 1 g dietary fiber, 361 mg sodium.

Put a Lid on It

When using the indirect grilling method, as in the recipe above, resist the urge to peek at food under the grill hood. Every time you raise the cover, you let heat escape and add as much as 15 minutes to the grilling time. Let foods grill the minimum time given in the recipe before checking for doneness.

DINNER AT SUNSET

Hazelnut-Pesto Turkey Breast
(see recipe, *opposite*)

Steamed asparagus

Romaine salad with vinaigrette dressing

Crusty Italian bread

Spumoni ice cream and almond biscotti

HAZELNUT-PESTO TURKEY BREAST

Smoked turkey breast at its flavorful best! Pesto melts under the skin during grilling, while the smoke from aromatic wood chips adds flavor throughout.

PREPARATION TIME: 40 MINUTES • GRILLING TIME: 1 TO 1½ HOURS

4	cups apple or cherry wood chips
¼	cup chopped hazelnuts or almonds, toasted (see tip, *page 87*)
1	egg yolk
1	cup loosely packed fresh spinach leaves
1	cup loosely packed fresh basil leaves
1	tablespoon hazelnut oil, almond oil, or cooking oil
1	clove garlic, minced
¼	cup grated Parmesan or Romano cheese
1	2½- to 3-pound fresh turkey breast half with bone
	Cooking oil

◆ **Cover** wood chips with water; soak at least 1 hour before grilling.

◆ **For pesto,** place hazelnuts or almonds in a blender container or food processor bowl; cover and blend or process until very finely chopped. Add egg yolk, spinach, basil, the 1 tablespoon oil, and the garlic. Cover; blend or process until nearly smooth. If necessary, stop processor and scrape container sides. Stir in the Parmesan or Romano cheese.

◆ **Remove** bone from turkey, if desired. To loosen turkey skin, slip fingers under, leaving skin attached at one long edge. Spread the pesto over the meat under the skin. Fold the skin over pesto. Secure with wooden skewers or toothpicks. If bone is removed, tuck thinner portion of breast under thicker portion; tie with string. Insert a meat thermometer into the thickest portion of turkey breast, without touching bone, if present.

◆ **Drain** wood chips. In a covered grill, arrange *medium-hot* coals around a drip pan. Pour 1 inch of water into drip pan. Sprinkle *half* of the wood chips onto the coals. Test for *medium* heat above the pan. Place turkey breast, pesto-stuffed side up, on the grill rack over the drip pan but not over the coals. Brush skin with cooking oil.

◆ **Cover** and grill until meat thermometer registers 170°, allowing 1 to 1¼ hours for breast with bone and about 1½ hours for boneless breast. During grilling, add more coals, drained wood chips, and water as necessary. Remove turkey from grill; let turkey stand, covered, for 10 minutes before slicing. Makes 6 to 8 servings.

NUTRITION FACTS PER SERVING: 266 cal., 38 g pro., 2 g carbo., 11 g fat, 120 mg chol., 1 g dietary fiber, 151 mg sodium.

GRILLED CHICKEN AND VEGETABLE SALAD

PREPARATION TIME. 15 MINUTES • GRILLING TIME: 17 TO 20 MINUTES

  1 cup sliced cauliflower or broccoli flowerets
  1 cup fresh baby carrots
  1 medium red and/or yellow sweet pepper, cut into strips
  1 small red onion, thinly sliced and separated into rings
 ½ cup bottled honey-mustard salad dressing
  4 skinless, boneless chicken breast halves (about 1 pound total)
  6 cups torn mixed greens
1½ cups cherry tomatoes, halved
     Bottled honey-mustard salad dressing (optional)

◆ **Tear off** two 24x18-inch pieces of heavy foil. Make a double thickness of foil that measures 24x18 inches. Place cauliflower, carrots, pepper, and onion in center of foil. Pour ¼ *cup* of the salad dressing over vegetables and toss to coat. Bring up 2 opposite edges of the foil; seal with a double fold. Then fold in the remaining ends to completely enclose the vegetables, leaving space for steam to build.

◆ **Grill** foil packet on the rack of an uncovered grill directly over medium coals for 5 minutes.

◆ **Rinse** chicken; pat dry. Brush chicken with remaining ¼ cup salad dressing. Place chicken on the grill rack directly over *medium* coals next to the vegetable packet. Grill, uncovered, for 12 to 15 minutes or until chicken is tender and no longer pink, turning once halfway through grilling time.

◆ **To serve,** arrange salad greens and tomatoes on individual plates. Diagonally cut the chicken pieces into slices; reassemble breast halves over greens. Divide vegetables among the plates. Drizzle salad with additional dressing, if desired. Makes 4 servings.

NUTRITION FACTS PER SERVING: 303 cal., 29 g pro., 25 g carbo., 10 g fat, 72 mg chol., 3 g dietary fiber, 276 mg sodium.

GREENS GALORE

The supermarket produce section is brimming with packaged mixed greens, ready to toss right out of the bag and into salads. Mixed greens typically come in 10- or 16-ounce packages. Use this guide for choosing the correct amount for recipes:
◆ **10-ounce package = approximately 8 to 9 cups greens**
◆ **16-ounce package = approximately 12 cups greens**

ZESTY DRUMSTICKS

Keep these ingredients in your pantry for a quick, spicy-sweet sauce.

PREPARATION TIME: 15 MINUTES • GRILLING TIME: 35 TO 45 MINUTES

- ¼ cup currant jelly
- ¼ cup chili sauce
- 1 tablespoon vinegar
- 1 tablespoon Worcestershire sauce
- ⅛ teaspoon garlic powder
  Several dashes bottled hot pepper sauce
- 8 chicken drumsticks (about 1½ pounds total)

◆ **For sauce,** combine all ingredients *except* chicken drumsticks in a small saucepan. Cook over low heat about 5 minutes or until bubbly, stirring occasionally to melt jelly. Remove from heat; set aside.

◆ **Remove** skin from chicken, if desired. Rinse chicken; pat dry.

◆ **Grill** chicken on the rack of an uncovered grill directly over *medium* coals for 35 to 45 minutes or until chicken is tender and no longer pink, turning once halfway through grilling time and brushing with sauce frequently during the last 10 minutes of grilling. Makes 4 servings.

NUTRITION FACTS PER SERVING (SKIN ON): 295 cal., 29 g pro., 18 g carbo., 12 g fat, 95 mg chol., 0 g dietary fiber, 370 mg sodium.

BRUSHING WITH SAUCES

As recommended in the recipe above, brush on sweet sauces during the last 10 to 15 minutes of grilling. This allows the flavor of the sauce to penetrate into the food without burning.

CAJUN CHICKEN

The mildly seasoned sauce is also delicious served over grilled vegetables.

PREPARATION TIME: 15 MINUTES • GRILLING TIME: 35 TO 40 MINUTES

1 2½- to 3-pound broiler-fryer chicken, quartered or cut up
1 14½-ounce can Cajun-style stewed tomatoes, cut up
1 tablespoon cornstarch
2 tablespoons balsamic vinegar
1 cup chopped zucchini and/or yellow summer squash
1 tablespoon snipped fresh basil

◆ **Rinse** chicken; pat dry. If using quartered chicken, break wing, hip, and drumstick joints so the pieces will lie flat during cooking. Twist wing tips under backs. Sprinkle chicken lightly with salt and pepper. Place chicken, bone side up, on the rack of an uncovered grill directly over *medium* coals. Grill for 20 minutes.

◆ **Meanwhile,** combine *undrained* tomatoes and cornstarch in a medium saucepan. Cook and stir over medium-high heat until thickened and bubbly; cook and stir for 2 minutes more. Stir in vinegar. Remove half of the sauce mixture; set aside to use as a brush-on sauce. Stir squash into remaining mixture in saucepan; cook for 2 minutes more. Remove from heat and set aside.

◆ **Turn** chicken and grill for 15 to 25 minutes more or until chicken is tender and no longer pink. Brush the chicken with the brush-on sauce frequently during the last 10 to 15 minutes of grilling.

◆ **Reheat** the tomato-squash mixture in saucepan. Stir in basil and spoon over chicken. Makes 4 servings.

NUTRITION FACTS PER SERVING: 299 cal., 30 g pro., 11 g carbo., 15 g fat, 94 mg chol., 2 g dietary fiber, 452 mg sodium.

POULTRY SAFETY POINTERS

◆ **Never thaw poultry on the countertop or in the sink, because bacteria can develop on poultry at room temperature. Thaw it in the refrigerator.**
◆ **Wash your hands, utensils, cutting boards, and work surfaces with hot soapy water after handling poultry to prevent spreading bacteria to other foods.**
◆ **Use separate dishes for raw and cooked poultry.**

SOUTHERN HOSPITALITY

Cajun Chicken
(see recipe, *opposite*)

Grilled Summer Vegetables
(see recipe, *pages 70-71*)

Buttered corn on the cob

Blueberry pie à la mode

MESQUITE GRILLED CHICKEN SANDWICHES

Try toasting the buns on the grill. Place, cut side down, on a grill rack directly over the coals. Grill, uncovered, 1 minute or until toasted.

PREPARATION TIME: 15 MINUTES • GRILLING TIME: 5 TO 7 MINUTES

	Mesquite wood chunks or chips
¼	cup nonfat mayonnaise or salad dressing
1	teaspoon white wine Worcestershire sauce
½	teaspoon finely shredded lime or lemon peel
4	skinless, boneless chicken breast halves (about 1 pound total)
2	tablespoons white wine Worcestershire sauce
¼	to ½ teaspoon garlic pepper seasoning
⅛	teaspoon salt
½	cup shredded part-skim mozzarella cheese (2 ounces)
4	whole wheat hamburger buns or hard rolls, split and toasted
4	slices tomato
½	of a large ripe avocado, halved, seeded, peeled, and thinly sliced

◆ **Cover** wood chunks or chips with water and soak for at least 1 hour before grilling.

◆ **Meanwhile,** for lime mayonnaise, combine mayonnaise or salad dressing, the 1 teaspoon Worcestershire sauce, and the lime or lemon peel in a small mixing bowl. Cover and chill.

◆ **Rinse** chicken; pat dry. Place each chicken piece between 2 pieces of plastic wrap; pound with flat side of a meat mallet to flatten slightly (about ½ inch thick). Remove plastic wrap. Brush both sides of chicken with the 2 tablespoons Worcestershire sauce; sprinkle with garlic pepper seasoning and salt.

◆ **Drain** wood chunks or chips. Sprinkle wet chunks or chips over *medium* coals. Grill chicken on the rack of an uncovered grill directly over *medium* coals for 5 to 7 minutes or until chicken is tender and no longer pink, turning once halfway through grilling time. Sprinkle each piece of chicken with cheese; grill just until cheese is melted.

◆ **To serve,** spread the cut side of bottom halves of buns with mayonnaise mixture. Place cooked chicken on top. Top each with more mayonnaise mixture, a tomato slice, 1 to 2 avocado slices, and top halves of buns. Makes 4 servings.

NUTRITION FACTS PER SERVING: 330 cal., 29 g pro., 28 g carbo., 11 g fat, 67 mg chol., 2 g dietary fiber, 695 mg sodium.

TANDOORI CHICKEN

In this traditional Indian dish, the spicy marinade is tamed by the smooth tartness of plain yogurt.

PREPARATION TIME: 15 MINUTES • MARINATING TIME: 6 TO 24 HOURS • GRILLING TIME: 50 TO 60 MINUTES

    1   8-ounce carton plain yogurt
    2   tablespoons lemon juice
    2   teaspoons grated gingerroot or ¾ teaspoon ground ginger
    1   teaspoon ground coriander
    ½   teaspoon ground cumin
    ¼   teaspoon ground turmeric
    ⅛   teaspoon ground red pepper
    1   clove garlic, minced
    4   chicken breast halves (about 1½ pounds total)

◆ **For marinade,** combine yogurt, lemon juice, gingerroot, coriander, cumin, turmeric, red pepper and garlic in a small mixing bowl.

◆ **Remove** skin from chicken, if desired. Rinse chicken; pat dry. Place chicken in a heavy plastic bag set into a deep bowl. Pour marinade over chicken in bag. Seal bag and turn chicken to coat. Marinate in refrigerator for 6 to 24 hours, turning bag occasionally. Remove chicken from bag; reserve marinade. Chill reserved marinade while grilling chicken.

◆ **In a covered grill** arrange *medium-hot* coals around a drip pan. Test for *medium* heat above the pan. Place chicken, bone side down, on the grill rack over the drip pan but not over the coals. Cover and grill for 50 to 60 minutes or until chicken is tender and no longer pink, brushing with marinade during the last 10 minutes of grilling. Makes 4 servings.

NUTRITION FACTS PER SERVING (SKIN ON): 293 cal., 41 g pro., 6 g carbo., 11 g fat, 111 mg chol., 0 g dietary fiber, 131 mg sodium.

TEMPERATURE CONTROL

To maintain the proper temperature during indirect grilling, you'll need to add additional briquettes to the grill. Depending on the size of your grill, add 5 to 10 briquettes to each side of the firebox every hour as needed. Or, consult your grill manufacturer's instructions.

**BEST-OF-SUMMER
BARBECUE**

*Grilled Chicken
Salad with
Plum Vinaigrette*
(see recipe, *opposite*)

*Steamed green
beans and
julienne carrots*

Sourdough rolls

*Raspberry sorbet
with crisp
sugar cookies*

GRILLED CHICKEN SALAD WITH PLUM VINAIGRETTE

Grilling brings out the natural sweetness of fresh plums. Serve on the skewers for a beautiful presentation.

PREPARATION TIME: 30 MINUTES • GRILLING TIME: 8 TO 10 MINUTES

⅓ cup white wine vinegar
¼ cup bottled plum sauce, plum preserves, or sweet-and-sour sauce
3 tablespoons salad oil
¼ teaspoon ground coriander
¼ teaspoon coarsely ground black pepper
1 pound skinless, boneless chicken breasts, cut into 2x1-inch strips
4 medium plums
1 cup pea pods, halved crosswise
6 cups torn mixed greens, such as romaine or red leaf lettuce

◆ **Soak** sixteen 5- to 6-inch-long wooden skewers in water for 30 minutes.

◆ **For vinaigrette,** combine vinegar; plum sauce, preserves, or sweet-and-sour sauce; oil; coriander; and pepper in a small mixing bowl. Reserve ¼ cup for brushing sauce; set aside remaining vinaigrette for salad dressing.

◆ **Thread** chicken strips accordion-style onto 8 skewers. Cut each plum into 8 wedges; thread onto remaining 8 skewers.

◆ **Grill** skewered chicken on the rack of an uncovered grill directly over *medium-hot* coals for 8 to 10 minutes or until chicken is tender and no longer pink, adding the skewered plums during the last 3 minutes and brushing occasionally with the ¼ cup plum vinaigrette.

◆ **Meanwhile,** cook pea pods, covered, in a small amount of boiling water for 2 to 4 minutes or until crisp-tender. (Or, place pea pods and 2 tablespoons *water* in a 1-quart microwave-safe casserole. Micro-cook, covered, on 100% power [high] for 2 to 2½ minutes or until crisp-tender.) Drain.

◆ **To serve,** toss together pea pods and greens in a large bowl. Arrange pea pod mixture, chicken, and plums on 4 dinner plates. Serve with remaining plum vinaigrette. Serves 4.

NUTRITION FACTS PER SERVING: 300 cal., 26 g pro., 21 g carbo., 15 g fat, 59 mg chol., 4 g dietary fiber, 101 mg sodium.

TURKEY WITH GINGER SALSA

Add Oriental and Mexican spice to your meal by marinating turkey breasts in a ginger-flavored sauce, which also flavors the tomato salsa.

PREPARATION TIME: 25 MINUTES • MARINATING TIME: 1 HOUR • GRILLING TIME: 12 TO 15 MINUTES

¼	cup vinegar
2	tablespoons dry sherry
2	tablespoons soy sauce
1	tablespoon grated gingerroot
1	clove garlic, minced
1	teaspoon seeded and finely chopped dried red chili pepper or
	1 teaspoon crushed red pepper
4	turkey breast tenderloin steaks (about 1 pound total)
1	medium tomato, peeled, seeded, and chopped
1	green onion, sliced
¼	cup chopped green pepper
1	tablespoon chopped fresh cilantro
4	6-inch flour tortillas (optional)
	Snipped fresh cilantro (optional)

◆ **For marinade,** combine vinegar, sherry, soy sauce, gingerroot, garlic, and red pepper. Set *2 tablespoons* of mixture aside.

◆ **Rinse** turkey; pat dry. Place turkey in a heavy plastic bag set into a shallow dish. Pour remaining marinade over turkey in bag. Seal bag; turn turkey to coat well. Marinate in the refrigerator for 1 hour, turning once.

◆ **For salsa,** combine reserved marinade, tomato, green onion, green pepper, and the 1 tablespoon cilantro in a bowl. Cover and chill until serving time.

◆ **Drain** turkey, reserving marinade. Grill turkey on the rack of an uncovered grill directly over *medium* coals for 12 to 15 minutes or until turkey is tender and no longer pink, turning once halfway through grilling time and brushing often with the reserved marinade.

◆ **To heat tortillas,** if using, place in a single layer on the grill rack about 1 minute. Serve turkey with chilled salsa and, if desired, warm tortillas. Garnish with additional fresh cilantro, if desired. Serves 4.

NUTRITION FACTS PER SERVING: 145 cal., 27 g pro., 5 g carbo., 1 g fat, 71 mg chol., 1 g dietary fiber, 563 mg sodium.

SOUTHWESTERN-STYLE BURGERS

PREPARATION TIME: 20 MINUTES • GRILLING TIME: 16 TO 20 MINUTES

  1 beaten egg
  ¼ cup crushed nacho-flavored or plain tortilla chips (1 ounce)
  3 tablespoons finely chopped green pepper
  ¾ teaspoon chili powder
  ¼ teaspoon salt
  ¼ teaspoon pepper
  1 pound ground raw chicken or turkey
  1 medium ripe avocado, halved, seeded, peeled, and sliced
  4 ounces sliced Monterey Jack cheese with jalapeño peppers
  4 kaiser rolls or hamburger buns, split
     Lettuce leaves
     Salsa

◆ **Combine** egg, tortilla chips, green pepper, chili powder, salt, and pepper in a medium mixing bowl. Add ground chicken and mix well. Shape into four ¾-inch-thick patties.

◆ **Grill** patties on the rack of an uncovered grill directly over *medium-hot* coals for 15 to 18 minutes or until no longer pink, turning once halfway through grilling time. Top each patty with avocado slices and cheese. Grill 1 to 2 minutes more or until cheese is melted. Toast rolls or buns on grill, if desired (see recipe blurb, *page 22*).

◆ **To serve,** place one lettuce leaf on bottom half of each bun. Top with cooked burgers and salsa. Makes 4 servings.

Hawaiian Chicken Burgers: Prepare meat mixture as above, *except* substitute ¼ cup *fine dry seasoned bread crumbs* for the tortilla chips; 3 tablespoons chopped *water chestnuts* for the green pepper; and ¾ teaspoon *ground ginger* for the chili powder.

◆ **Grill** patties as above, *except* brush with ¼ cup *bottled sweet-and-sour sauce* during last 5 minutes of grilling. Place *fresh or canned pineapple slices* on grill rack during the last 5 minutes of cooking, if desired. Toast rolls or buns on grill, if desired (see recipe blurb, *page 22*).

◆ **To serve,** sprinkle bottom half of each bun with some shredded *spinach.* Top with patties. Brush patties with sweet-and-sour sauce and top with pineapple slices, if desired. Makes 4 servings.

NUTRITION FACTS PER SERVING OF SOUTHWESTERN-STYLE BURGERS: 424 cal., 29 g pro., 26 g carbo., 23 g fat, 133 mg chol., 2 g dietary fiber, 674 mg sodium.

Beef, Lamb, & Pork

The aroma of juicy, tender burgers and steaks on the grill is so hard to resist, it's no wonder that Americans barbecue these foods more than any other. Turn to this chapter to tempt your taste buds and expand your grilling repertoire with mouthwatering specialties such as Sonoma Grilled Lamb, Tequila-Lime Fajitas, and Honey-Orange Pork Chops.

Herb-Rubbed Steaks
(see recipe, *page 30*)

HERB-RUBBED STEAKS

A juicy steak, grilled to perfection, remains one of America's best-loved classics. Pictured on pages 28-29.

PREPARATION TIME: 15 MINUTES • GRILLING TIME: 12 TO 22 MINUTES

1	1- to 1½-pound boneless beef sirloin steak, cut 1 to 1½ inches thick
¼	cup finely chopped onion
2	cloves garlic, minced
1	teaspoon dried herb (such as thyme, basil, oregano, or rosemary)
¼	teaspoon salt
⅛	teaspoon pepper
	Bottled barbecue sauce (optional)

◆ **Trim** fat from steak. Combine onion, garlic, herb, salt, and pepper in a small mixing bowl. Sprinkle evenly over both sides of meat; rub in with your fingers.

◆ **Grill** steak on the rack of an uncovered grill directly over *medium* coals to desired doneness, turning once halfway through grilling time. For medium doneness, allow 12 to 15 minutes total for a 1-inch-thick steak; 18 to 22 minutes total for 1½-inch-thick steak. During cooking, brush steak occasionally with barbecue sauce, if desired. Makes 4 to 6 servings.

NUTRITION FACTS PER SERVING: 136 cal., 20 g pro., 2 g carbo., 5 g fat, 57 mg chol., 0 g dietary fiber, 176 mg sodium.

LET COLOR BE YOUR GUIDE

Learn to judge the doneness of steaks and chops by referring to the visual color checks below. Start by making a small slit near the bone. For boneless cuts of meat, make a slit near the center.

◆ **Medium-rare (145°): Meat is pink in the center with the very outer portion brown—not recommended for pork chops.**

◆ **Medium (160°): Meat is light pink in the center with a brown outer portion.**

◆ **Well-done (180°): Meat is brown throughout, with no pink color remaining.**

TEQUILA-LIME FAJITAS

Grill the fajita fixin's along with the steak. Even the tortillas can be heated on the grill, keeping your kitchen cool.

PREPARATION TIME: 20 MINUTES • MARINATING TIME: 6 TO 24 HOURS • GRILLING TIME: 12 TO 14 MINUTES

- ½   cup lime juice
- ¼   cup tequila
- ¼   cup cooking oil
- 1   4-ounce can chopped green chili peppers, drained
- ½   teaspoon bottled hot pepper sauce
- ¼   teaspoon salt
- 1   pound boneless beef flank steak or beef plate skirt steak
- 1   medium onion, thinly sliced
- 8   8-inch flour or corn tortillas
- ⅔   cup salsa (optional)
- 1   medium ripe avocado, pitted, peeled, and sliced (optional)
- ½   cup dairy sour cream (optional)

◆ **For marinade,** combine lime juice, tequila, cooking oil, green chili peppers, bottled hot pepper sauce, and salt in a medium mixing bowl.

◆ **Place** steak and onion in a heavy plastic bag set into a shallow dish. Pour marinade over steak in bag. Seal bag; turn steak to coat well. Marinate in the refrigerator for 6 to 24 hours, turning bag occasionally. Remove steak from bag; reserve marinade.

◆ **Tear** off a 36x18-inch piece of heavy foil. Fold in half to make a double thickness of foil that measures 18x18 inches. Using a slotted spoon, remove onion and green chili peppers from marinade and place in center of foil. Bring up 2 opposite edges of foil; seal with a double fold. Then fold in remaining ends to completely enclose the onions and peppers, leaving space for steam to build.

◆ **Stack** the tortillas and wrap in a double thickness of heavy foil.

◆ **Grill** steak and the wrapped onion and chili peppers on the rack of an uncovered grill directly over *medium* coals for 6 minutes. Turn steak and brush with reserved marinade. Add wrapped tortillas to the grill rack. Continue grilling for 6 to 8 minutes more for medium doneness of steak.

◆ **Thinly slice** steak into bite-size strips. Divide steak, onion, and chili peppers among the tortillas. Roll up tortillas. Top with salsa and serve with avocado slices and sour cream, if desired. Makes 4 servings.

NUTRITION FACTS PER SERVING: 581 cal., 30 g pro., 46 g carbo., 27 g fat, 57 mg chol., 3 g dietary fiber, 880 mg sodium.

A TASTE OF THAILAND SUPPER

Thai Steak and Pasta Salad with Peanut-Pepper Dressing
(see recipe, *opposite*)

Iced tea

Frozen vanilla yogurt sprinkled with chopped crystallized ginger

Fortune cookies

THAI STEAK AND PASTA SALAD WITH PEANUT-PEPPER DRESSING

Lemongrass, a lemon-flavored herb, gives this salad its authentic Thai flavor.

PREPARATION TIME: 25 MINUTES • MARINATING TIME: 30 MINUTES TO 2 HOURS •
GRILLING TIME: 12 TO 15 MINUTES

     4 ounces fine noodles or fusilli pasta, broken (2½ cups)
    ⅓ cup rice wine vinegar or vinegar
    ⅓ cup salad oil
     3 tablespoons soy sauce
     2 tablespoons peanut butter
     1 tablespoon chopped fresh lemongrass or snipped fresh cilantro
     2 cloves garlic, minced
    ¼ teaspoon crushed red pepper
     1 pound boneless beef top sirloin steak, cut 1 inch thick
     5 cups shredded savoy or Chinese cabbage, spinach, romaine, and/or bok choy
    ½ cup shredded carrot
     4 green onions, cut lengthwise into fourths and bias-sliced into 1-inch pieces
    ½ of a medium cucumber, sliced
     1 medium yellow summer squash, cut into thin strips
    ¼ cup chopped peanuts

◆ **Cook** noodles according to package directions; drain, cover, and chill.

◆ **For dressing,** place vinegar, salad oil, soy sauce, peanut butter, lemongrass or cilantro, garlic, and crushed red pepper in a blender container or food processor bowl. Cover and blend or process until mixture is combined.

◆ **Trim** excess fat from meat; place meat in a shallow dish. Add *⅓ cup* of the dressing; turn once. Cover; marinate in the refrigerator for 2 hours or let stand at room temperature for 30 minutes. Refrigerate remaining dressing until ready to serve.

◆ **Drain** meat, discarding marinade. Grill steak on the rack of an uncovered grill directly over *medium* coals for 12 to 15 minutes for medium doneness, turning once halfway through grilling time. Cut into thin strips.

◆ **Meanwhile,** combine noodles, cabbage, carrot, and green onions. Add about ¼ *cup* of the remaining dressing; toss to coat well. Arrange the noodle mixture on 4 salad plates; top with meat, cucumber, and squash. Drizzle with remaining dressing; sprinkle with chopped peanuts. Garnish each serving with whole fresh red hot chili peppers, if desired. Serves 4.

NUTRITION FACTS PER SERVING: 478 cal., 36 g pro., 33 g carbo., 24 g fat, 101 mg chol., 4 g dietary fiber, 536 mg sodium.

STUFFED SIRLOIN WITH MIXED MUSHROOM SAUTÉ

Fresh exotic mushrooms are becoming more widely available. Our suggested trio gives this delicious recipe a rich, earthy flavor.

PREPARATION TIME: 25 MINUTES • GRILLING TIME: 18 TO 22 MINUTES

	Onion Stuffing (see recipe, *below*)
1	2-pound boneless beef top sirloin steak, cut 1½ inches thick
1½	cups sliced mixed fresh mushrooms (such as shiitake, oyster, and brown mushrooms)
1	tablespoon margarine or butter
¾	cup beef broth
2	teaspoons cornstarch
2	teaspoons Worcestershire sauce
2	tablespoons dry red wine
1	tablespoon snipped parsley

◆ **Prepare** onion stuffing for steak. To make a pocket in steak, use a sharp paring knife and make a short horizontal slit in 1 side of steak. Insert knife into slit, drawing from side to side to form a larger pocket in steak. Spoon stuffing into pocket. Close the pocket with wooden picks inserted diagonally.

◆ **For mushroom sauce,** cook mushrooms in margarine or butter in a large skillet until tender. Combine beef broth, cornstarch, and Worcestershire sauce in a medium bowl; carefully add to skillet. Cook and stir until thickened and bubbly; cook and stir for 2 minutes more. Stir in wine and parsley. Keep warm while grilling steak.

◆ **Grill** steak on the rack of an uncovered grill directly over *medium-hot* coals for 18 to 22 minutes for medium doneness, turning once halfway through grilling time. Serve with mushroom sauce. Makes 6 to 8 servings.

◆ **Onion Stuffing:** Cook 1 small *onion,* halved, sliced, and separated into rings, and 1 clove *garlic,* minced, in 1 tablespoon *margarine* or *butter* in a large skillet until onion is tender but not brown. Stir in ¼ teaspoon *lemon-pepper seasoning.*

NUTRITION FACTS PER SERVING: 253 cal., 31 g pro., 3 g carbo., 12 g fat, 88 mg chol., 0 g dietary fiber, 254 mg sodium.

TEXAS BARBECUE BEEF

A zesty brush-on sauce and serve-along Soppin' Sauce guarantee the big, bold taste that Texans—and many non-Texans—love in their barbecue.

PREPARATION TIME: 15 MINUTES • GRILLING TIME: 12 TO 14 MINUTES

¼ cup Worcestershire sauce
3 tablespoons vinegar
1 teaspoon ground cumin
1 teaspoon dry mustard
½ teaspoon bottled hot pepper sauce
¼ teaspoon ground cinnamon
1 1½-pound beef flank steak or round steak, cut about ¾ inch thick
  Soppin' Sauce (see recipe, *below*) or purchased barbecue sauce

◆ **For brush-on sauce,** combine Worcestershire sauce, vinegar, cumin, dry mustard, hot pepper sauce, and cinnamon in a small bowl.

◆ **Grill** steak on the rack of an uncovered grill directly over *medium* coals for 12 to 14 minutes for medium doneness, turning once halfway through grilling time and brushing frequently with brush-on sauce. Remove meat from the grill and allow to stand, covered loosely with foil, about 10 minutes for easier carving. To serve, thinly slice the meat across the grain. Serve with Soppin' Sauce. Makes 6 servings.

◆ **Soppin' Sauce:** Combine ½ cup *catsup,* ¼ cup *water,* 2 tablespoons finely chopped *onion,* 2 tablespoons *apple jelly,* 1 tablespoon *vinegar,* 1 tablespoon *Worcestershire sauce,* ⅛ teaspoon *salt,* and 1 *jalapeño pepper,* seeded and finely chopped (see tip, *page 59*), in a small saucepan. On the grill or stove top, bring the sauce to boiling. (If grilling, bring sauce to boiling over direct heat, then place over indirect heat to simmer.) Simmer, uncovered, about 15 minutes or to desired consistency.

NUTRITION FACTS PER SERVING WITH SOPPIN' SAUCE: 232 cal., 24 g pro., 14 g carbo., 9 g fat, 57 mg chol., 1 g dietary fiber, 521 mg sodium.

CLEANING YOUR GRILL RACK

If you don't have a stiff-bristled brush for cleaning the grill rack, crumble some foil. While the rack is still warm, use an oven mitt or glove to protect your hand and wipe away baked-on food. Then discard the foil.

STEAK AND SPINACH PINWHEELS

Impress your guests with round steak filled with a delectable spinach-and-Parmesan stuffing.

PREPARATION TIME: 25 MINUTES • GRILLING TIME: 12 TO 14 MINUTES

8	slices bacon
1	1- to 1½-pound boneless beef top round steak
1	10-ounce package frozen chopped spinach, thawed and well drained
¼	cup grated Parmesan cheese

◆ **Cook** bacon in a large skillet just until done but not crisp. Drain on paper towels.

◆ **Score** steak by making shallow cuts at 1-inch intervals diagonally across the steak in a diamond pattern. Repeat on second side. Place meat between 2 sheets of plastic wrap. With the flat side of a meat mallet, pound the steak into a 12x8-inch rectangle, working from the center to the edges. Remove plastic wrap. Sprinkle steak with salt and pepper. Arrange bacon lengthwise on steak.

◆ **Spread** spinach over bacon. Sprinkle with Parmesan cheese. Roll up from a short side. Secure with wooden toothpicks at 1-inch intervals, starting ½ inch from one end. Cut between toothpicks into eight 1-inch slices. Thread 2 slices onto each of 4 long skewers.

◆ **Grill** steak slices on the rack of an uncovered grill directly over *medium* coals for 12 to 14 minutes for medium doneness, turning once halfway through grilling time. Remove toothpicks and skewers. Makes 4 servings.

NUTRITION FACTS PER SERVING: 274 cal., 36 g pro., 4 g carbo., 12 g fat, 87 mg chol., 2 g dietary fiber, 431 mg sodium.

TIP FOR TURNING MEAT

Always use tongs or a large spatula for turning meat on the grill. Then you'll avoid piercing the meat, which causes it to lose its natural juices.

DINNER
ON THE DECK

*Steak and Spinach
Pinwheels*
(see recipe, *opposite*)

Rice and orzo pilaf

Steamed asparagus

*Summertime
Fruit Trifle*
(see recipe, *page 91*)

ZESTY STEAK CARBONNADE

Carbonnade is a French term for meat cooked over hot coals; salsa catsup provides a Mexican counterpoint.

PREPARATION TIME: 40 MINUTES • MARINATING TIME: 1 TO 24 HOURS • GRILLING TIME: 12 TO 15 MINUTES

⅔	cup beer
½	cup chopped onion
⅓	cup salsa catsup or catsup
2	tablespoons sugar
4	teaspoons lemon juice
1	tablespoon Worcestershire sauce
½	teaspoon paprika
½	teaspoon chili powder
¼	teaspoon pepper
6	top loin steaks, cut 1 inch thick (about 2 pounds total)

◆ **For marinade,** combine all ingredients *except* steak in a small saucepan. Bring to boiling; reduce heat. Simmer, uncovered, for 5 minutes. Cool.

◆ **Score** meat by making shallow cuts at 1-inch intervals diagonally across the steaks in a diamond pattern. Place steaks in a heavy plastic bag set into a shallow dish. Pour marinade over steaks. Seal bag and turn steaks to coat. Marinate in the refrigerator for at least 1 hour or up to 24 hours, turning bag occasionally.

◆ **Remove** steaks from bag; reserve marinade. Grill steaks on the rack of an uncovered grill directly over *medium-hot* coals for 12 to 15 minutes for medium doneness, turning once halfway through grilling.

◆ **Meanwhile,** place reserved marinade in a small saucepan; bring to a full boil. Cook and stir for 1 to 2 minutes. Serve with steaks. Makes 6 servings.

NUTRITION FACTS PER SERVING: 283 cal., 35 g pro., 11 g carbo., 10 g fat, 101 mg chol., 1 g dietary fiber, 282 mg sodium.

PLAY-IT-SAFE CUTTING

Designate one cutting board for scoring and trimming raw meat, poultry, or fish. Do not use this board for cutting vegetables or slicing bread. After each use, wash all cutting boards in hot, soapy water or in the dishwasher. Also, remember to transfer cooked meat, fish, or poultry from the grill to a clean plate using clean utensils.

LEMON-DILL MARINATED FLANK STEAK

PREPARATION TIME: 20 MINUTES • MARINATING TIME: 6 TO 24 HOURS • GRILLING TIME: 12 TO 14 MINUTES

- 1   1- to 1½-pound beef flank steak, cut about ¾ inch thick
- ¼   cup sliced green onions
- ¼   cup water
- ¼   cup dry red wine
- ¼   cup reduced-sodium or regular soy sauce
- 3   tablespoons lemon juice
- 2   tablespoons cooking oil
- 1   tablespoon snipped fresh dill or 1 teaspoon dried dillweed
- 1   tablespoon reduced-sodium or regular Worcestershire sauce
- 2   cloves garlic, minced
- ½   teaspoon celery seed
- ½   teaspoon pepper

◆ **Score** meat by making shallow cuts at 1-inch intervals diagonally across the steak in a diamond pattern. Repeat scoring on the second side. Place meat in a heavy plastic bag set into a shallow dish.

◆ **For marinade,** combine green onions, water, red wine, soy sauce, lemon juice, cooking oil, dill, Worcestershire sauce, garlic, celery seed, and pepper in a medium mixing bowl. Pour marinade over steak in bag. Seal bag; turn steak to coat well. Marinate in the refrigerator for 6 to 24 hours, turning the bag occasionally.

◆ **Remove** steak from bag; reserve marinade. Grill steak on the rack of an uncovered grill directly over *medium* coals for 12 to 14 minutes for medium doneness, turning once halfway through grilling time and brushing occasionally with the reserved marinade. To serve, thinly slice meat across the grain. Makes 6 servings.

NUTRITION FACTS PER SERVING: 138 cal., 17 g pro., 2 g carbo., 7 g fat, 38 mg chol., 0 g dietary fiber, 232 mg sodium.

MARINATE LIKE MAGIC

There are several advantages for using heavy plastic bags for marinating. First, less marinade is needed. Distributing the marinade over the food is easy—instead of stirring the food, just turn the sealed bag occasionally. And, cleanup is a snap—just throw away the messy bag.

PICNIC AT THE PARK

Grilled Burgers Italiano
(see recipe, *opposite*)

Sliced tomato salad with red wine vinaigrette

Carrot and celery sticks

Mocha chip ice cream

GRILLED BURGERS ITALIANO

The quintessential summertime favorite—a big, juicy burger—takes on the flavors of Italy.
For directions on toasting the kaiser rolls, see recipe blurb, page 22. Pictured on the cover.

PREPARATION TIME: 25 MINUTES • GRILLING TIME: 10 TO 12 MINUTES

1	beaten egg
¼	cup meatless spaghetti sauce
⅓	cup fine dry bread crumbs
⅓	cup chopped onion
3	tablespoons snipped fresh basil or oregano, or 1 teaspoon dried basil or oregano, crushed
2	cloves garlic, minced
1	pound lean ground beef
1	pound bulk Italian sausage
2	medium green, yellow, and/or red sweet peppers, cut into rings and halved
1	tablespoon olive oil or cooking oil
1	6-ounce package sliced mozzarella cheese, halved crosswise
1	cup meatless spaghetti sauce
8	kaiser rolls, split and toasted

◆ **Combine** egg and the ¼ cup spaghetti sauce in a large mixing bowl. Stir in bread crumbs, onion, basil or oregano, and garlic. Add beef and sausage; mix well. Shape meat mixture into eight ½-inch-thick patties.

◆ **Tear** off a 12x18-inch piece of heavy foil. Place pepper slices in center of foil; drizzle with oil. Bring up 2 opposite edges of foil; seal with a double fold. Then fold in remaining ends to enclose the peppers, leaving space for steam to build.

◆ **Grill** burgers and foil packet on the rack of an uncovered grill directly over *medium* coals for 10 to 12 minutes or until burgers are no longer pink and peppers are tender, turning burgers and foil packet once halfway through grilling time.

◆ **Top** each burger with some of the pepper strips and a half slice of cheese; cover and grill about 15 seconds more or until cheese melts.

◆ **Meanwhile,** heat the 1 cup spaghetti sauce either on the grill or stove top. To serve, place burgers on kaiser rolls. Spoon spaghetti sauce over burgers. Pass any remaining sauce. Makes 8 servings.

NUTRITION FACTS PER SERVING: 540 cal., 31 g pro., 41 g carbo., 27 g fat, 106 mg chol., 0 g dietary fiber, 995 mg sodium.

SWEET ONION MARINATED BEEF ROAST

For a sweeter simmered onion mixture, start with sweet onions such as Vidalia.

PREPARATION TIME: 20 MINUTES • MARINATING TIME: 24 HOURS • GRILLING TIME: 1½ HOURS

 ½ cup dry white wine
  2 tablespoons olive oil or cooking oil
  1 teaspoon dried dillweed
 ½ to 1 teaspoon coarse ground black pepper
  1 2- to 2½-pound beef eye of round roast, trimmed of fat
  2 medium onions, thinly sliced and separated into rings (2 cups)
    Dilled Horseradish Sauce (see recipe, *below*)

◆ **For marinade,** combine wine, oil, dillweed, pepper, and ¼ teaspoon *salt* in a small bowl. Place beef roast and onions in heavy plastic bag set into a deep bowl. Pour marinade over beef and onions. Marinate in the refrigerator for 24 hours, turning meat several times. Remove meat from bag; reserve marinade and onions.

◆ **In a covered grill** arrange *medium-hot* coals around a drip pan. Test for *medium* heat above the pan. Insert a meat thermometer into the roast. Place roast on the grill rack over the drip pan but not over the coals. Cover and grill roast about 1½ hours or until a thermometer registers 140°. Remove roast from grill. Cover meat loosely with foil and let stand about 15 minutes. The meat temperature will rise to 145° for medium-rare.

◆ **Meanwhile,** bring onions and marinade to boiling in a 10-inch skillet. Reduce heat and simmer, covered, for 10 to 12 minutes or until onions are tender. Thinly slice the roast and serve hot with the onion mixture and Dilled Horseradish Sauce. Makes 6 to 8 servings.

◆ **Dilled Horseradish Sauce:** In a small bowl, stir together ½ cup *mayonnaise,* ¼ cup *dairy sour cream,* 1 tablespoon *prepared horseradish,* and ½ teaspoon *dried dillweed.* Add salt and pepper to taste. Cover; chill until serving time.

NUTRITION FACTS PER SERVING: 420 cal., 34 g pro., 5 g carbo., 28 g fat, 93 mg chol., 1 g dietary fiber, 295 mg sodium.

GARLIC-HERB BREAD

Cut one 16-ounce loaf *French bread* crosswise into 1-inch-thick slices, cutting to but not through bottom crust. Spread cut surfaces with mixture of ½ cup softened *butter* or *margarine,* 2 cloves *garlic,* minced, and 1 tablespoon snipped fresh or 1 teaspoon dried *basil* or *oregano,* crushed. Wrap loaf in heavy foil and warm on the grill for 15 minutes.

SUMMER
CELEBRATION
SUPPER

*Sweet Onion
Marinated
Beef Roast*
(see recipe, *opposite*)

*Grilled Vegetables
Mediterranean*
(see recipe, *page 74*)

Garlic-Herb Bread
(see tip, *opposite*)

*Fresh strawberries
with whipped cream*

MOROCCAN-STYLE LAMB CHOPS

PREPARATION TIME: 25 MINUTES • MARINATING TIME: 24 HOURS • GRILLING TIME: 12 TO 16 MINUTES

¾	cup plain yogurt
3	tablespoons orange juice
2	tablespoons sliced green onion
1½	teaspoons ground coriander
½	teaspoon salt
½	teaspoon ground cumin
½	teaspoon ground cardamom
¼	teaspoon ground cinnamon
¼	teaspoon ground cloves
¼	teaspoon ground ginger
8	lamb leg sirloin chops, cut 1 inch thick
1	medium onion, chopped
1	medium tomato, chopped
1	medium cucumber, chopped
½	cup plain yogurt
	Hot cooked couscous or rice (optional)

◆ **For marinade,** combine the ¾ cup yogurt, orange juice, green onion, coriander, salt, cumin, cardamom, cinnamon, cloves, and ginger. Place chops in a shallow dish. Pour marinade over chops; turn to coat. Cover; marinate in refrigerator overnight, turning chops occasionally.

◆ **For sauce,** combine onion, tomato, and cucumber in a medium bowl; stir in the ½ cup yogurt. Season to taste with salt and pepper. Cover and chill until serving time.

◆ **Remove** chops from marinade, reserving as much marinade as possible. Grill on the rack of an uncovered grill directly over *medium* coals for 14 to 16 minutes for medium doneness, turning once halfway through grilling time and brushing often with marinade.

◆ **To serve,** arrange chops on plates with couscous or rice, if desired. Pass sauce. Serves 4.

Moroccan-Style Pork Chops: Prepare recipe as directed above, *except* substitute 6 *pork loin rib chops,* cut ¾ inch thick, for the lamb chops. Grill chops on the rack of an uncovered grill directly over *medium-hot* coals for 6 to 8 minutes or until no longer pink, turning once halfway through grilling time and brushing often with marinade. Makes 6 servings.

NUTRITION FACTS PER SERVING FOR LAMB CHOPS: 421 cal., 53 g pro., 12 g carbo., 17 g fat, 160 mg chol., 2 g dietary fiber, 443 mg sodium.

SONOMA GRILLED LAMB

Savor the eclectic flavors of sunny California in this company-special dish.

PREPARATION TIME: 20 MINUTES • MARINATING TIME: 8 TO 24 HOURS • GRILLING TIME: 40 TO 60 MINUTES

½ cup olive oil or cooking oil
⅓ cup red wine vinegar
⅓ cup dry red wine or chicken broth
1 4-ounce can chopped green chili peppers
2 tablespoons hot mustard
4 teaspoons dried Italian seasoning, crushed
4 cloves garlic, minced
1 3- to 4-pound leg of lamb, boned and butterflied*
1 8-ounce can tomato sauce
3 tablespoons honey

◆ **For marinade,** combine oil, vinegar, wine or chicken broth, *undrained* chili peppers, mustard, Italian seasoning, and garlic in a small mixing bowl; mix well.

◆ **Remove** fell (paper-thin, pinkish-red layer) from outer surface of lamb; trim fat from lamb. Place lamb in a large heavy plastic bag set into a deep bowl. Pour marinade over meat in bag, turning to coat all sides. Marinate in the refrigerator for 8 hours or overnight, turning once. Remove lamb from marinade, reserving *½ cup* of the marinade for the basting sauce.

◆ **For basting sauce,** stir together reserved marinade, tomato sauce, and honey.

◆ **In a covered grill** arrange *medium* coals around a drip pan. Test for *medium-slow* heat above the pan. Insert a meat thermometer into the lamb. Place the lamb, fat side up, on the grill rack over the drip pan but not over the coals. Cover and grill for 40 to 60 minutes or until thermometer registers 140°. During the last 10 minutes of grilling, brush frequently with the basting sauce. Remove meat from grill. Cover meat loosely with foil and let stand about 15 minutes. The meat temperature will rise to 145° for medium-rare.

◆ **Heat** any remaining basting sauce to a full boil in a small saucepan. Cook for 1 minute. Pass with meat. Makes 8 servings.

◆ ***Note:** When purchasing the leg of lamb for Sonoma Grilled Lamb, have your butcher bone it for you. The 3- to 4-pound weight given *above* is with the bone in.

NUTRITION FACTS PER SERVING: 290 cal., 21 g pro., 10 g carbo., 19 g fat, 72 mg chol., 1 g dietary fiber, 324 mg sodium.

MEDITERRANEAN-STYLE GRILL-OUT

Rosemary Lamb Kabobs
(see recipe, *opposite*)

Mixed greens salad with balsamic vinaigrette

Couscous with chopped tomato

Cantaloupe or casaba wedges with rainbow sherbet

ROSEMARY LAMB KABOBS

Partially precooking the carrots and zucchini before grilling helps ensure they'll be properly cooked when the meat is done.

PREPARATION TIME: 20 MINUTES • MARINATING TIME: 4 HOURS • GRILLING TIME: 12 TO 14 MINUTES

¾ cup white grape juice
2 tablespoons olive oil or cooking oil
2 tablespoons lime juice
1½ teaspoons snipped fresh rosemary or ½ teaspoon dried rosemary, crushed
2 cloves garlic, minced
⅛ teaspoon ground cinnamon
1 pound boneless lamb round steak or sirloin chops, cut into 1-inch cubes
2 cups fresh baby carrots (about ½ pound)
2 medium zucchini or yellow summer squash, sliced ½ to ¾ inch thick
1 large green or red sweet pepper, cut into 1-inch pieces
Fresh rosemary sprigs (optional)

◆ **For marinade,** combine grape juice, oil, lime juice, rosemary, garlic, and cinnamon in a medium mixing bowl. Place lamb cubes in a heavy plastic bag set in a shallow dish. Pour marinade over lamb in bag. Seal bag; turn to coat. Marinate in the refrigerator for 4 hours, turning once to distribute marinade. Remove lamb cubes from bag; reserve marinade.

◆ **Trim** carrots, leaving ½ to 1 inch of stem, if desired. Scrub but do not peel. Cook carrots in a small amount of boiling water for 3 minutes. Add zucchini or summer squash and cook for 1 to 2 minutes more or until vegetables are crisp-tender. Drain.

◆ **Alternately** thread lamb cubes, whole carrots, zucchini or summer squash, and green or red sweet pepper on eight 8-inch skewers.

◆ **Grill** kabobs on the rack of an uncovered grill directly over *medium* coals for 12 to 14 minutes for medium doneness, brushing with reserved marinade and turning kabobs occasionally. Garnish with fresh rosemary sprigs, if desired. Makes 4 servings.

NUTRITION FACTS PER SERVING: 283 cal., 26 g pro., 12 g carbo., 15 g fat, 78 mg chol., 3 g dietary fiber, 84 mg sodium.

JUST-RIGHT KABOBS

Leave a small space (about ¼ inch) between each piece of food on the skewer to ensure even grilling.

SPICED AND SMOKED RIBS

Pork ribs get triple flavor when rubbed with spices, cooked with smoke, and slathered with Molasses Glaze.

PREPARATION TIME: 50 MINUTES • GRILLING TIME: 45 TO 50 MINUTES

  4 cups hickory chips
  4 pounds pork loin back ribs or meaty pork spareribs
  1 tablespoon brown sugar
  1 teaspoon five-spice powder
  ½ teaspoon salt
  ½ teaspoon paprika
  ¼ teaspoon celery seed
  ¼ teaspoon pepper
     Molasses Glaze (see recipe, *below*)

◆ **Cover** wood chips with water; soak at least 1 hour before grilling.

◆ **Cut** the pork ribs into serving-size pieces (portions with 3 to 4 ribs each). Place in a Dutch oven. Add enough water to cover ribs. Bring to boiling; reduce heat. Simmer, covered, for 30 minutes. Drain. Cool the ribs slightly.

◆ **Combine** brown sugar, five-spice powder, salt, paprika, celery seed, and pepper in a small bowl. When ribs are cool enough to handle, rub spice mixture over ribs.

◆ **Drain** wood chips. In a covered grill arrange *medium-slow* coals around a drip pan. Pour 1 inch of water into the drip pan. Place drained wood chips onto the coals. Test for *slow* heat above the pan. Place ribs on grill rack over the drip pan but not over the coals. Cover and grill for 30 minutes.

◆ **Meanwhile,** prepare Molasses Glaze. Brush glaze on ribs after the 30 minutes of grilling time. Grill for 15 to 20 minutes more or until ribs are tender and no pink remains, brushing with glaze occasionally. Makes 4 servings.

◆ **Molasses Glaze:** Stir together ½ cup *catsup,* 2 tablespoons *light molasses,* 1 tablespoon *lemon juice,* 1 tablespoon *soy sauce,* and several dashes *bottled hot pepper sauce* in a small bowl. Use to brush on ribs during the last 15 to 20 minutes of grilling.

NUTRITION FACTS PER SERVING WITH MOLASSES GLAZE: 340 cal., 30 g pro., 19 g carbo., 16 g fat, 97 mg chol., 1 g dietary fiber, 963 mg sodium.

JULY 4TH SIZZLER

Spiced and Smoked Ribs
(see recipe, *opposite*)

Chilled watermelon slices

Deli coleslaw

Baked beans

Hot fudge sundaes

SINGAPORE SATAY

Lean pork is the perfect partner for the Southeast Asian flavors in the curry marinade and the accompanying spicy peanut-butter sauce.

PREPARATION TIME: 20 MINUTES • MARINATING TIME: 1 TO 2 HOURS • GRILLING TIME: 10 TO 12 MINUTES

¼	cup soy sauce
2	tablespoons cooking oil
2	tablespoons lemon juice
1	tablespoon toasted sesame oil
1	tablespoon honey
1	teaspoon curry powder
1	clove garlic, minced
12	ounces lean boneless pork
4	to 5 tablespoons hot water
¼	cup peanut butter
1	green onion, chopped
½	teaspoon grated gingerroot
	Dash ground red pepper
2	cups hot cooked rice

◆ **For marinade,** combine soy sauce, cooking oil, lemon juice, toasted sesame oil, honey, curry powder, and garlic.

◆ **Trim** fat from meat. Cut meat into long slices about ¼ inch thick. Place meat in a heavy plastic bag set into a deep bowl. Pour marinade over pork in bag. Seal bag; turn to coat meat well. Marinate in the refrigerator for 1 to 2 hours, turning bag occasionally.

◆ **For sauce,** in a small bowl gradually stir hot water into peanut butter until smooth and of a sauce consistency. Stir in green onion, gingerroot, and red pepper. Set aside.

◆ **Remove** pork from bag; reserve marinade. Thread pork slices, accordion style, onto 4 long skewers, leaving about ¼ inch between pieces. Grill kabobs on the grill rack of an uncovered grill directly over *medium* coals for 10 to 12 minutes or until pork is done and juices run clear, turning once and brushing with reserved marinade halfway through grilling time.

◆ **To serve,** arrange kabobs over rice. Serve with sauce. Serves 4.

NUTRITION FACTS PER SERVING: 356 cal., 19 g pro., 29 g carbo., 19 g fat, 38 mg chol., 1 g dietary fiber, 564 mg sodium.

RED-HOT BRATS IN BEER

Boil the bratwurst first in a spicy beer mixture, then chill overnight for a quick-grilling meal the next day.

PREPARATION TIME: 35 MINUTES • GRILLING TIME: 7 TO 8 MINUTES

    6   fresh (uncooked) bratwursts (about 1¼ pounds total)
    2   12-ounce cans (3 cups) beer
    1   tablespoon bottled hot pepper sauce
    1   tablespoon Worcestershire sauce
    2   teaspoons ground red pepper
    1   teaspoon chili powder
    6   frankfurter buns, split
        Sauerkraut (optional)
        Pickles (optional)
        Mustard (optional)

◆ **Prick** several holes in the skin of each bratwurst.

◆ **Combine** the bratwursts, beer, hot pepper sauce, Worcestershire sauce, red pepper, and chili powder in a large saucepan.

◆ **Bring** to boiling; reduce heat. Simmer, covered, about 20 minutes or until bratwursts are no longer pink. Drain. Cover and chill until ready to grill.

◆ **Grill** bratwursts on the rack of an uncovered grill directly over *medium-hot* coals for 7 to 8 minutes or until the bratwurst skins are golden, turning frequently. Serve bratwursts on buns. Top with sauerkraut, pickles, and mustard, if desired. Makes 6 servings.

NUTRITION FACTS PER SERVING: 290 cal., 13 g pro., 24 g carbo., 15 g fat, 44 mg chol., 2 g dietary fiber, 1,070 mg sodium.

ZESTY RELISH FOR BRATS

Try topping plain grilled bratwursts with this sweet and tangy Pepper Pear Relish: Combine ¾ cup *cider vinegar,* ⅔ cup chopped peeled *pear,* ½ cup finely chopped *red sweet pepper,* ½ cup finely chopped *onion,* one 4-ounce can diced *green chili peppers* (drained), ¼ cup *sugar,* 2 teaspoons prepared *mustard,* and ⅛ teaspoon ground *turmeric* in a medium saucepan. Bring to boiling; reduce heat. Simmer, uncovered, for 30 minutes or until most of the liquid has evaporated, stirring occasionally. Transfer relish to a storage container. Cover and chill up to 4 days. Makes 1 cup.

SAVORY SUMMERTIME SUPPER

Honey-Orange Pork Chops with acini de pepe stuffing
(see recipe, *opposite*)

Stir-fried sugar snap peas

Whole wheat rolls

Rhubarb crisp with vanilla ice cream

HONEY-ORANGE PORK CHOPS

PREPARATION TIME: 25 MINUTES • GRILLING TIME: 35 TO 40 MINUTES

    2   medium oranges
    2   tablespoons honey
    1   tablespoon Dijon-style mustard
    2   tablespoons orange marmalade
    2   tablespoons vinegar
   ¾   cup chicken broth
   ½   cup acini de pepe
    4   green onions, thinly sliced
   ¼   teaspoon ground ginger
   ½   cup finely chopped celery
    4   pork loin rib chops, cut 1¼ inches thick

◆ **Peel,** section, and seed the oranges, reserving juices; coarsely chop the orange sections. For glaze, combine honey and mustard in a small saucepan. Stir in orange marmalade and vinegar. Heat and stir until the marmalade melts. Remove from heat; set aside.

◆ **For stuffing,** bring broth to boiling in a saucepan; add acini de pepe, onions, and ginger. Reduce heat; simmer, uncovered, 5 minutes or until acini de pepe is tender. Remove from heat. Fold in orange sections, *2 tablespoons* reserved juice, *2 tablespoons* of the glaze, and celery.

◆ **Cut** a pocket in each pork chop by cutting from the fat side almost to the bone. Spoon *2 to 3 tablespoons* stuffing into each chop. Fasten pockets with a wooden toothpick. Spoon remaining stuffing onto a large sheet of double thickness of foil. Bring up 2 opposite edges of foil; seal with a double fold. Then fold in remaining ends to completely enclose stuffing, leaving space for steam to build. Set aside.

◆ **In a covered grill** arrange *medium-hot* coals around a drip pan. Test for *medium* heat above the pan. Place stuffed pork chops on the grill rack over the drip pan but not over the coals. Cover and grill for 20 minutes. Turn chops and brush with some of the honey glaze. Place the foil packet of stuffing on grill next to chops. Cover and grill for 15 to 20 minutes more or until the chops are done and juices run clear, brushing chops occasionally with remaining honey glaze. Remove toothpicks. Serve chops with extra stuffing. Serves 4.

NUTRITION FACTS PER SERVING: 296 cal., 23 g pro., 37 g carbo., 8 g fat, 51 mg chol., 2 g dietary fiber, 358 mg sodium.

PORK MEDALLIONS WITH SUMMER SALSA

PREPARATION TIME: 35 MINUTES • MARINATING TIME: 4 TO 24 HOURS • GRILLING TIME: 20 TO 30 MINUTES

    Summer Salsa (see recipe, *below*)
8   boneless pork loin chops, cut 1¼ to 1½ inches thick (America's Cut)
¼   cup lime juice
¼   cup Worcestershire sauce
¼   cup coarse-grain brown mustard or Dijon-style mustard
3   tablespoons vinegar
2   tablespoons water
1½ teaspoons ground cumin
¼   teaspoon salt
⅛   teaspoon pepper

◆ **Prepare** Summer Salsa; chill up to 4 hours, stirring occasionally.

◆ **Place** the pork chops in a heavy plastic bag set in a large bowl. Combine remaining ingredients in a medium bowl. Pour over pork in bag. Seal bag. Marinate in the refrigerator 4 to 24 hours, turning occasionally.

◆ **Remove** the pork from the bag; reserve marinade. Grill pork on the rack of an uncovered grill directly over *medium* coals for 20 to 30 minutes or until the chops are done and juices run clear, turning once halfway through cooking and brushing with marinade. Serve with Summer Salsa. Makes 8 servings.

NUTRITION FACTS PER SERVING: 248 cal., 25 g pro., 11 g carbo., 12 g fat, 77 mg chol., 182 mg sodium, 1 g dietary fiber.

◆ **Summer Salsa:** Combine 1½ cups chopped fresh *apricots* or peeled *peaches,* ¾ cup chopped *red* or *green sweet pepper*, ¾ cup chopped, seeded *cucumber*, ¼ cup sliced *green onions*, 1 to 2 *jalapeño peppers,* seeded and finely chopped (see tip, *page 59*), 2 tablespoons *honey,* 2 tablespoons *lime juice,* and 1 tablespoon snipped fresh *cilantro* or *parsley* in a medium mixing bowl.

NUTRITION FACTS PER 3-TABLESPOON SERVING: 36 cal., 1 g pro., 9 g carbo., 0 g fat, 0 mg chol., 1 mg sodium, 1 g dietary fiber.

CAJUN-STYLE PORK CHOPS

Rubbing both sides of the pork chops with the pepper rub gives them plenty of flavor.

PREPARATION TIME: 10 MINUTES • GRILLING TIME: 25 TO 35 MINUTES

- 1 teaspoon onion powder
- ¼ to ½ teaspoon ground white pepper
- ¼ to ½ teaspoon ground red pepper
- ¼ to ½ teaspoon ground black pepper
- ¼ teaspoon salt
- 4 pork loin or rib chops, cut 1¼ to 1½ inches thick (about 2¼ pounds total)

◆ **For rub,** combine onion powder, ground white pepper, ground red pepper, ground black pepper, and salt in a small mixing bowl.

◆ **Trim** fat from meat. Rub both sides of each pork chop with the seasoning rub.

◆ **Grill** pork chops on the grill rack of an uncovered grill directly over *medium* coals for 25 to 35 minutes or until chops are done and juices run clear, turning once halfway through grilling time.

NUTRITION FACTS PER SERVING: 207 cal., 24 g pro., 1 g carbo., 11 g fat, 77 mg chol., 192 mg sodium, 0 g dietary fiber.

SIMPLE AND SAFE MARINATING

Marinades used on meat, poultry, or fish contain raw meat juices, so, if you plan to brush them on during cooking, do so during the early stages; that way, they'll have time to thoroughly cook. To serve marinade with meat, first bring the marinade to a full boil and cook and stir for 1 to 2 minutes. Discard any leftover marinade.

Orange-Glazed Shrimp Kabobs
(see recipe, *page 58*)

Fish & Seafood

For today's
health-conscious and
fast-paced lifestyles,
quick-cooking fish on the grill
is a natural. Whether
marinated with herbs or
served with a fresh chunky
salsa or a smooth sauce,
grilled fish and seafood are
wonderful ways to brighten
up and lighten up your
summertime meals.

Orange-Glazed Shrimp Kabobs

A four-ingredient glaze flavors these colorful kabobs. Pictured on pages 56–57.

PREPARATION TIME: 25 MINUTES • GRILLING TIME: 6 TO 10 MINUTES

  1   pound fresh or frozen peeled and deveined medium to large shrimp
  ¼   cup bottled French salad dressing
  ¼   cup orange marmalade
  2   teaspoons grated gingerroot or ¾ teaspoon ground ginger
  2   teaspoons soy sauce
  ¼   of a fresh pineapple, cut into 16 small wedges
  1   small red pepper, cut into 16 pieces
      Fresh spinach leaves

◆ **Thaw** shrimp, if frozen. For sauce, stir together salad dressing, marmalade, gingerroot, and soy sauce in a small mixing bowl.

◆ **Thread** shrimp onto 8 short skewers. Thread pineapple and pepper pieces onto 4 long skewers. Grill shrimp on the greased rack of an uncovered grill directly over *medium* coals for 6 to 10 minutes or until shrimp are opaque on the inside, turning shrimp once halfway through grilling time and brushing with sauce during the last 2 minutes of grilling. Add pineapple and pepper skewers to the grill during the last 5 minutes of grilling, turning once and brushing with sauce halfway through grilling time.

◆ **Serve** skewers of shrimp, pineapple, and pepper on spinach leaves. Makes 4 servings.

NUTRITION FACTS PER SERVING: 210 cal., 14 g pro., 23 g carbo., 7 g fat, 120 mg chol., 1 g dietary fiber, 535 mg sodium.

Shrimp Savvy

Shrimp are sold by the pound. The price per pound usually is determined by the size—the bigger the shrimp, the higher the price and the fewer per pound. Refer to this guide when choosing shrimp.

Size Description	Average Count Per Pound	Direct Grilling Time (minutes)
Medium	20	6 to 8
Large	16 to 18	8 to 10
Jumbo	12 to 15	10 to 12

SWORDFISH WITH SALSA VERDE

Salsa verde or "green salsa," derives its color from classic Mexican ingredients: tomatillos, cilantro, avocados, and hot peppers.

PREPARATION TIME: 25 MINUTES • GRILLING TIME: 8 TO 12 MINUTES

5	or 6 fresh tomatillos (6 ounces), husks removed, and finely chopped, or one 13-ounce can tomatillos, drained, rinsed, and finely chopped
2	tablespoons finely chopped onion
2	serrano or jalapeño peppers, seeded and finely chopped
1	tablespoon snipped fresh cilantro or parsley
1	teaspoon finely shredded lime peel or grapefruit peel
½	teaspoon sugar
4	fresh or frozen swordfish or tuna steaks, cut ¾ to 1 inch thick (1¼ pounds total)
¼	teaspoon salt
¼	teaspoon ground cumin
¼	teaspoon ground black pepper
	Olive oil
½	of a medium ripe avocado, seeded, peeled, and coarsely chopped

◆ **For salsa verde,** stir together the tomatillos, onion, serrano or jalapeño peppers, cilantro or parsley, lime or grapefruit peel, and sugar in a nonmetallic mixing bowl. Set aside. (To make ahead, cover and chill for up to 2 days.)

◆ **Thaw** fish, if frozen. Combine salt, cumin, and black pepper. Brush fish with olive oil. Sprinkle with cumin mixture. Stir avocado into the salsa verde.

◆ **Grill** fish on the greased rack of an uncovered grill directly over *medium* coals for 8 to 12 minutes or just until fish begins to flake easily when tested with a fork, turning once halfway through grilling time. Serve with salsa verde. Makes 4 servings.

NUTRITION FACTS PER SERVING: 220 cal., 29 g pro., 5 g carbo., 10 g fat, 53 mg chol., 3 g dietary fiber, 321 mg sodium.

TOO HOT TO HANDLE

Hot peppers—such as jalapeño and serrano—contain oils that can burn your eyes, lips, and skin. When working with them, protect your hands with plastic bags or wear plastic gloves. And, be sure to wash your hands thoroughly before you touch your eyes or face.

SALMON FILLETS WITH ORANGE-BASIL SAUCE

A tangy orange sauce lends citrus-fresh flavor to the juicy salmon.

PREPARATION TIME: 15 MINUTES • GRILLING TIME: 8 TO 12 MINUTES

  6 4-ounce boneless, skinless fresh or frozen salmon fillets, cut 1 inch thick
  ¼ cup frozen orange juice concentrate, thawed
  3 tablespoons olive oil or cooking oil
  2 tablespoons snipped fresh basil or 2 teaspoons dried basil, crushed
  2 tablespoons water
  1 tablespoon snipped fresh mint or tarragon or 1 teaspoon dried mint or tarragon, crushed
  1 tablespoon Worcestershire sauce
  2 cloves garlic, minced
     Fresh mint or basil sprigs (optional)

◆ **Thaw** fish, if frozen. For sauce, combine concentrate, oil, the snipped basil, water, the snipped mint or tarragon, Worcestershire sauce, and garlic in a bowl.

◆ **Brush** salmon with sauce.

◆ **Grill** fish on the greased rack of an uncovered grill directly over *medium* coals for 8 to 12 minutes or just until salmon begins to flake easily when tested with a fork, turning once halfway through grilling time and brushing often with sauce. Garnish with mint or basil sprigs, if desired. Makes 6 servings.

NUTRITION FACTS PER SERVING: 284 cal., 25 g pro., 9 g carbo., 16 g fat, 74 mg chol., 1 g dietary fiber, 87 mg sodium.

USING A GRILL BASKET

Because fish is delicate and breaks apart easily, consider using a grill basket when grilling. Use a grill basket for direct cooking only; most grill basket handles can't take the heat of indirect cooking on a covered grill. Also, be sure to lightly grease the basket with cooking oil before adding the fish.

FLORIDA-STYLE BARBECUE

Salmon Fillets with Orange-Basil Sauce
(see recipe, *opposite*)

Spinach fettuccine

Grilled vegetable kabobs

Crusty hard rolls

Chilled lemon mousse

GARLIC-BUTTERED SHRIMP

You can also grill these garlicky shrimp on short bamboo skewers to make tempting appetizers that will serve 10 to 12 guests.

PREPARATION TIME: 20 MINUTES • GRILLING TIME: 6 TO 10 MINUTES

- 1 pound fresh or frozen peeled and deveined medium to large shrimp
- ¼ cup margarine or butter
- 1 clove garlic, minced
- 1 tablespoon snipped fresh parsley
  Dash ground red pepper
- 3 tablespoons dry white wine
  Shredded lettuce (optional)

◆ **Thaw** shrimp, if frozen. For sauce, melt margarine or butter in a small saucepan. Stir in garlic, parsley, and red pepper; cook for 1 minute. Stir in wine; heat through. Set aside.

◆ **Thread** shrimp onto 4 long or 8 short skewers. Grill on the greased rack of an uncovered grill directly over *medium* coals for 6 to 10 minutes or until shrimp are opaque on the inside, turning once halfway through grilling time and brushing frequently with sauce. Serve on a bed of shredded lettuce, if desired. Makes 4 servings.

NUTRITION FACTS PER SERVING: 195 cal., 19 g pro., 1 g carbo., 12 g fat, 166 mg chol., 0 g dietary fiber, 325 mg sodium.

NO-STICK TRICK

To prevent fish from sticking to the grill, brush the cold grill rack with oil, or spray with nonstick spray coating. To avoid flare-ups, don't spray over the hot coals.

GINGERED FISH FILLETS

For a light dinner, serve this elegant grilled fish entrée with a slice of crusty French bread and sparkling water. Other fish varieties that work well for this include cod, orange roughy, haddock, or pike.

PREPARATION TIME: 10 MINUTES • MARINATING TIME: 1 HOUR • GRILLING TIME: 6 TO 8 MINUTES

4	4-ounce fresh or frozen red snapper or whitefish fillets, cut ½ to ¾ inch thick
2	green onions, sliced
2	tablespoons olive oil or cooking oil
2	tablespoons rice vinegar or vinegar
1½	teaspoons grated gingerroot
1	teaspoon toasted sesame oil
1	medium tomato
1	small green pepper

◆ **Thaw** fish, if frozen. For marinade, combine green onions, oil, vinegar, gingerroot, and sesame oil in a small mixing bowl.

◆ **Place** fish in a heavy plastic bag set into a deep bowl. Pour marinade over fish in bag. Seal bag; turn fish to coat well. Marinate in the refrigerator for 1 hour, turning bag occasionally. Remove fish from bag; reserve marinade. Cut several slits in an 18x18-inch piece of heavy foil. Grease foil and place fish on it.

◆ **Cut** the tomato into wedges and the green pepper into rings. Thread tomato wedges onto 2 long metal skewers, leaving ¼ inch between pieces. Place peppers on the foil.

◆ **Place** foil with fish and peppers on the rack of an uncovered grill directly over *medium* coals. Grill for 4 minutes. Turn fish and brush with reserved marinade. Add tomato wedges. Grill for 2 to 4 minutes more or just until fish begins to flake easily when tested with a fork and the green pepper is crisp-tender. Makes 4 servings.

NUTRITION FACTS PER SERVING: 192 cal., 23 g pro., 3 g carbo., 10 g fat, 40 mg chol., 1 g dietary fiber, 53 mg sodium.

GRILLING FISH TO PERFECTION

Estimate grilling time for fish according to thickness. Allow 4 to 6 minutes for each one-half inch of thickness. Turn fish once during cooking by gently slipping a wide spatula under the fish for the best support.

EASY, ELEGANT COOKOUT

Rosemary-Marinated Swordfish
(see recipe, *opposite*)

Buttered baby carrots and fresh green beans

Belgian endive salad with red pepper vinaigrette

Garlic-Herb Bread
(see tip, *page 42*)

Peach melba compote

ROSEMARY-MARINATED SWORDFISH

A perfect light entrée for a warm summer evening. For extra herb flavor, use a sprig of fresh rosemary to brush on the marinade during grilling.

PREPARATION TIME: 10 MINUTES • MARINATING TIME: 2 HOURS • GRILLING TIME: 6 TO 9 MINUTES

4	4-ounce fresh or frozen swordfish, halibut, or tuna steaks, cut ¾ inch thick
2	green onions, thinly sliced
2	tablespoons white wine vinegar
1	tablespoon water
1	tablespoon olive oil or cooking oil
2	teaspoons snipped fresh rosemary or ½ teaspoon dried rosemary, crushed
1	teaspoon white wine Worcestershire sauce
⅛	teaspoon salt
	Dash pepper
	Fresh rosemary sprigs (optional)

◆ **Thaw** fish, if frozen. For marinade, combine green onions, vinegar, water, olive oil, the snipped rosemary, Worcestershire sauce, salt, and pepper in a shallow dish. Place fish steaks in dish; turn to coat. Cover and marinate in refrigerator for 2 hours, turning once.

◆ **Drain** fish, reserving marinade. Grill fish on the greased rack of an uncovered grill directly over *medium* coals for 4 minutes. Brush with marinade and turn fish over. Grill for 2 to 5 minutes more or just until fish begins to flake easily when tested with a fork. Spoon additional sliced green onion and snipped fresh rosemary over top, if desired. Garnish with fresh rosemary sprigs, if desired. Makes 4 servings.

NUTRITION FACTS PER SERVING: 170 cal., 23 g pro., 1 g carbo., 8 g fat, 45 mg chol., 0 g dietary fiber, 179 mg sodium.

MARINATING FISH

For the best results, limit the marinating time for fish steaks and fillets to no more than two hours. If the fish marinates longer, it will begin to toughen.

FISH STEAKS WITH FRESH FRUIT SALSA

Salsa with a sophisticated twist! Accent sweet, summer-ripe fruit with fresh hot peppers and herbs.

PREPARATION TIME: 25 MINUTES • GRILLING TIME: 8 TO 12 MINUTES

    4   fresh or frozen halibut, swordfish, shark, or salmon steaks, cut 1 inch thick
            (about 2 pounds total)
    ½   small ripe papaya, peeled, seeded, and chopped
    1   small ripe nectarine, pitted and chopped
    1   fresh jalapeño pepper, seeded and chopped* or 1 tablespoon capers, drained
    1   tablespoon snipped fresh rosemary, basil, or thyme
    1   tablespoon olive oil
        Olive oil

◆ **Thaw** fish, if frozen.

◆ **For fruit salsa,** several hours ahead, stir together the papaya, nectarine, jalapeño pepper or capers, snipped herb, and the 1 tablespoon olive oil in a medium bowl. Cover and chill thoroughly.

◆ **Brush** both sides of steaks with olive oil. Grill fish on the greased rack of an uncovered grill directly over *medium* coals for 8 to 12 minutes or just until fish begins to flake easily when tested with a fork, turning fish once and brushing with olive oil halfway through grilling time. Serve fish with the fruit salsa. Makes 4 servings.

◆ ***Note:** See tip on *page 59* for handling hot peppers.

NUTRITION FACTS PER SERVING: 300 cal., 46 g pro., 8 g carbo., 9 g fat, 0 mg chol., 2 g dietary fiber, 150 mg sodium.

FRESH AND FLAVORFUL FISH

Here are some quick and easy, low-fat ways to add flavor and variety to grilled fish:
◆ Use your favorite low-fat salad dressing as a marinade or brush-on sauce for grilled fish.
◆ Squeeze fresh lemon juice over grilled fish and sprinkle with fresh snipped basil.
◆ Stir together low-fat yogurt, shredded cucumber, and fresh snipped dill to spoon on top of grilled fish.

LIGHT-STYLE LUNCHEON

*Fish Steaks with
Fresh Fruit Salsa*
(see recipe, *opposite*)

*Steamed baby
summer squash*

Lemon-parsley rice

*Angel food cake with
raspberry sauce*

Extras

This summer, run the grilling gamut and sizzle up some surprises on your barbecue grill. Vegetables, quesadillas, even pizza are deliciously different when cooked over the coals. So move over meat! Get ready for some exciting extras you'll savor all summer long.

Grilled Summer Vegetables (see recipe, *pages 70-71*)

GRILLED SUMMER VEGETABLES

Brushed with olive oil and cooked until slightly charred, grilled vegetables make eye-catching and palate-pleasing summertime fare. Pictured on pages 68-69.

Asparagus spears
Baby carrots
Eggplant
Fennel
Sweet peppers
Leeks
New potatoes
Baby zucchini or regular zucchini
Scallopini squash
Olive oil, melted margarine, or melted butter

◆ **Before grilling,** rinse vegetables. Trim, cut up, and precook vegetables as directed in chart on opposite page. To precook any one vegetable, bring a small amount of water to boiling in a medium saucepan; add desired vegetable and simmer, covered, for the time specified in chart. Drain well.

◆ **To grill,** generously brush vegetables with olive oil, margarine, or butter before grilling. (Lay vegetables perpendicular to wires on grill rack so vegetables won't fall into coals.) Grill vegetables on the rack of an uncovered grill directly over *medium-hot* coals until tender and slightly charred, following the timings in chart and turning occasionally.

NUTRITION FACTS PER SERVING (1 NEW POTATO, 1 BABY CARROT, 5 ASPARAGUS SPEARS BRUSHED WITH 1 TABLESPOON OLIVE OIL): 203 cal., 3 g pro., 18 g carbo., 14 g fat, 0 mg chol., 2 g dietary fiber, 16 mg sodium.

MORE GREAT GRILLED VEGETABLES

Try these quick tips, using leftover grilled vegetables, for adding variety, nutrition, and flavor to your everyday meals:

◆ Combine with marinara or pasta sauce.

◆ Arrange on top of an Italian bread shell (Boboli brand).

◆ Add to soups and stews.

◆ Stir into a rice pilaf.

◆ Roll up in a flour tortilla.

Timings for Grilled Vegetables

Vegetable	Preparation	Precooking Time	Grilling Time
Asparagus	Snap off and discard tough bases of stems. Precook, then tie asparagus in bundles with strips of cooked green onion tops.	3 to 4 minutes	3 to 5 minutes
Baby Carrots	Cut off tops. Wash and peel.	3 to 5 minutes	3 to 5 minutes
Eggplant	Cut off top and blossom ends. Cut eggplant crosswise into 1-inch-thick slices.	Do not precook.	8 minutes
Fennel	Snip off feathery leaves. Cut off stems. Precook, then cut bulbs into 6 to 8 wedges.	Precook whole bulbs 10 minutes.	8 minutes
Sweet Peppers	Remove stem. Quarter peppers. Remove seeds and membranes. Cut peppers into 1-inch-wide strips.	Do not precook.	8 to 10 minutes
Leeks	Cut off green tops; trim bulb roots and remove 1 to 2 layers of white skin. Precook, then halve lengthwise.	10 minutes or until tender	5 minutes
New Potatoes	Halve potatoes.	10 minutes or until almost tender	10 to 12 minutes
Baby or Regular Zucchini	Wash; cut off ends. Quarter lengthwise into long strips.	Do not precook.	5 to 6 minutes
Scallopini Squash	Rinse and trim ends.	Precook whole squash for 3 minutes.	20 minutes

71

GRILLED QUESADILLAS

PREPARATION TIME: 8 MINUTES • GRILLING TIME: 3 TO 4 MINUTES

  6 7-inch flour tortillas
  2 tablespoons cooking oil
 ½ cup salsa
1½ cups shredded Monterey Jack cheese with jalapeño peppers (6 ounces)
     Dairy sour cream, guacamole, and/or salsa

◆ **Brush** 1 side of *three* of the tortillas with some of the cooking oil. Place tortillas, oil side down, on a large baking sheet. Spread salsa over each tortilla on baking sheet. Sprinkle each with cheese. Top with remaining tortillas. Brush top of tortillas with remaining oil.

◆ **Transfer** quesadillas to the grill rack of an uncovered grill directly over *medium* coals. Grill 3 to 4 minutes or until cheese begins to melt and tortillas start to brown, turning once halfway through grilling. Cut quesadillas into wedges. Top each with some sour cream, guacamole, and/or salsa. Garnish with cilantro, if desired. Makes 6 appetizer servings.

NUTRITION FACTS PER SERVING: 286 cal., 10 g pro., 20 g carbo., 18 g fat, 32 mg chol., 1 g dietary fiber, 424 mg sodium.

CARAMELIZED ONION AND CHEESE BITES

PREPARATION TIME: 20 MINUTES • GRILLING TIME: 2 MINUTES

     Caramelized Onion Topper (see recipe, *below*)
16 ¼-inch-thick slices baguette French bread or other long, thin, firm bread
 ½ cup freshly grated Parmesan or Romano cheese

◆ **Prepare** Caramelized Onion Topper. Spoon some of the topper on each of the bread slices. Sprinkle with the cheese.

◆ **Grill** bread slices, onion side up, on the rack of an uncovered grill directly over *medium-hot* coals about 2 minutes or just until bottoms are toasted and slices are heated through. Watch bread slices carefully the last 30 seconds to avoid overbrowning. Makes 8 servings.

◆ **Caramelized Onion Topper:** Cook 1 large *onion,* halved and thinly sliced, in 1 tablespoon hot *olive* or *cooking oil* in a large skillet about 3 minutes or just until tender. Add ⅓ cup coarsely chopped *walnuts* and 1 teaspoon *sugar.* Continue to cook and stir 5 minutes more or until the onion is slightly caramelized and walnuts are lightly toasted. Stir in 1 tablespoon *Dijon-style mustard.*

NUTRITION FACTS PER SERVING: 183 cal., 7 g pro., 22 g carbo., 8 g fat, 5 mg chol., 1 g dietary fiber, 378 mg sodium.

GRILLED VEGETABLES MEDITERRANEAN

For a delicious combination, serve with Sweet Onion Marinated Beef Roast (see recipe, page 42). Grill the vegetables first, then toss with the dried tomato vinaigrette while the roast cooks over the coals.

PREPARATION TIME: 40 MINUTES • GRILLING TIME: 10 MINUTES

3	dried tomatoes (dry packed)
1	medium eggplant (peel, if desired), sliced ¾ inch thick
1	fresh medium tomato, halved
1	medium onion, thickly sliced (½ inch)
1	medium green pepper, halved and seeded
2	tablespoons olive oil or cooking oil
1	clove garlic, minced
2	tablespoons red wine vinegar
1	tablespoon snipped parsley
1	tablespoon olive oil or cooking oil
⅛	teaspoon salt
	Dash pepper

◆ **Soak** dried tomatoes in boiling water for 2 minutes. Drain, finely chop, and set aside.

◆ **Brush** cut surfaces of sliced eggplant, halved fresh tomato, sliced onion, and halved green pepper with the 2 tablespoons olive or cooking oil. Grill vegetables on the rack of an uncovered grill directly over *hot* coals about 10 minutes or until crisp-tender and charred, turning once halfway through grilling time.

◆ **Remove** peel from pepper and skin tomato. Coarsely chop grilled vegetables and combine in a large bowl.

◆ **For vinaigrette,** stir together the rehydrated tomatoes, garlic, vinegar, parsley, the 1 tablespoon olive or cooking oil, the salt, and pepper in a small bowl. Stir vinaigrette into vegetable mixture. If making ahead, chill, covered. Remove from refrigerator 1 hour before serving to bring to room temperature. Makes 6 side-dish servings.

NUTRITION FACTS PER SERVING: 96 cal., 1 g pro., 8 g carbo., 7 g fat, 0 mg chol., 3 g dietary fiber, 54 mg sodium.

GRILLED TOMATOES WITH PESTO

Pick plump, vine-ripened tomatoes from your garden or farmer's produce stand for a true taste of summer.

PREPARATION TIME: 20 MINUTES • GRILLING TIME: 15 TO 20 MINUTES

3   medium tomatoes, cored, halved crosswise, at room temperature
2   tablespoons purchased pesto
6   very thin onion slices
½   cup shredded Monterey Jack cheese (2 ounces)
⅓   cup smoked almonds, chopped
2   tablespoons snipped parsley
    Parsley sprigs (optional)

◆ **Hollow** out the top ¼ inch of tomato halves, using a spoon. Top each tomato half with *1 teaspoon* of pesto and *one* onion slice. Arrange tomatoes in 2 foil pie plates.

◆ **In a covered grill** arrange *medium-hot* coals around the edges. Test for *medium* heat in the center of the grill. Place the foil pans containing the tomatoes on the center of the grill rack, but not over the coals. Cover and grill for 10 to 15 minutes or until the tomato halves are heated through.

◆ **Stir** together cheese, almonds, and snipped parsley in a small mixing bowl. Sprinkle over tomatoes. Cover and grill about 5 minutes more or until cheese is melted. Season to taste with salt and pepper. Garnish with parsley sprigs, if desired. Makes 6 side-dish servings.

NUTRITION FACTS PER SERVING: 133 cal., 5 g pro., 7 g carbo., 10 g fat, 9 mg chol., 2 g dietary fiber, 98 mg sodium.

A LITTLE PESTO CAN GO A LONG WAY

Consider using leftover purchased pesto as a topping on the Grilled Pizza (see recipe, page 80). For storage over a long time, spoon the pesto into ice-cube trays and freeze. Then pop the blocks of pesto out and place them in a freezer bag. Store them in the freezer up to 1 month. This lets you use only as many blocks as needed.

SOUTHWESTERN GRILLED CORN

Brush corn on the cob with cilantro-flecked melted margarine. For even more bite, sprinkle with additional ground red pepper to taste.

PREPARATION TIME: 15 MINUTES • GRILLING TIME: 20 MINUTES

⅓ cup margarine or butter
2 tablespoons snipped fresh cilantro or parsley
¼ teaspoon salt
¼ teaspoon ground red pepper
6 fresh ears of corn

◆ **Melt** margarine or butter in a small saucepan. Stir in cilantro or parsley, salt, and ground red pepper.

◆ **Remove** the husks from fresh ears of corn; scrub with a stiff brush to remove silks. Rinse ears; pat dry with paper towels. Place each ear of corn on a piece of heavy foil. Brush ears with margarine mixture. Wrap corn securely with foil.

◆ **Grill** corn on the rack of an uncovered grill directly over *medium-hot* coals about 20 minutes or until tender, turning frequently. Makes 6 side-dish servings.

NUTRITION FACTS PER SERVING: 173 cal., 3 g pro., 20 g carbo., 11 g fat, 0 mg chol., 4 g dietary fiber, 187 mg sodium.

FIESTA GRILLED PEPPERS

Grilled sweet peppers add smoky-mellow flavor to any barbecued meal. Use this simple preparation when your coal temperature is medium-slow.

PREPARATION TIME: 20 MINUTES • GRILLING TIME: 15 MINUTES

8 to 10 green, yellow, and/or red sweet peppers, quartered
2 to 3 tablespoons olive oil or cooking oil

◆ **Remove** seeds and membranes of peppers. Brush skins with oil. Grill, skin side down, on the rack of an uncovered grill directly over *medium-slow* coals about 15 minutes or until crisp-tender and charred. Makes 12 side-dish servings.

NUTRITION FACTS PER SERVING: 33 cal., 0 g pro., 3 g carbo., 2 g fat, 0 mg chol., 1 g dietary fiber, 1 mg sodium.

HOBO VEGETABLES

When you're looking for a basic buttered vegetable to serve with grilled meat, poultry, or fish, give these grilled packets a try.

PREPARATION TIME: 20 MINUTES • GRILLING TIME: 25 MINUTES

4   medium potatoes, thinly sliced
2   medium red onions, cut into thin wedges
2   medium carrots, cut into thin strips
¼   cup margarine or butter, melted
1   clove garlic, minced
½   teaspoon salt
¼   teaspoon pepper
2   tablespoons snipped parsley (optional)

◆ **Tear** off six 18x12-inch pieces of heavy foil. Divide potatoes, onions, and carrots evenly among pieces of foil, placing vegetables in center of each piece.

◆ **Stir** together margarine or butter, garlic, salt, and pepper in a small bowl. Brush mixture over vegetables in each packet, using all of the mixture. Bring up 2 opposite edges of foil; seal with a double fold. Then fold in remaining ends to completely enclose the vegetables, leaving space for steam to build.

◆ **Grill** foil packets on the rack of an uncovered grill directly over *medium* coals about 25 minutes or until vegetables are tender, turning packets over halfway through grilling time. Serve in the foil packets or transfer the vegetables to a serving platter. Sprinkle with parsley, if desired. Makes 6 side-dish servings.

NUTRITION FACTS PER SERVING: 186 cal., 3 g pro., 28 g carbo., 8 g fat, 0 mg chol., 2 g dietary fiber, 289 mg sodium.

IT'S A WRAP

Preparing side dishes in foil packets is a slick trick that helps you make the best use of your grill. Just place the packet alongside the meat as it cooks. If the meat takes longer to cook than the packet, keep the prepared packet in the refrigerator until it's time to add it to the grill. You may need to add a few extra minutes of grilling time to make sure that the chilled side dish is thoroughly heated. After grilling, be sure to open the foil packets carefully—the steam that builds in the sealed packet is very hot.

New Potatoes with Roasted Garlic

Garlic fans will enjoy the mellow roasted flavor in this warm potato salad.

PREPARATION TIME: 35 MINUTES • GRILLING TIME: 35 MINUTES

2	pounds tiny new potatoes, sliced
4	large cloves garlic (unpeeled)
1	tablespoon olive oil or cooking oil
¼	teaspoon salt
2	tablespoons snipped chives
1	tablespoon olive oil or cooking oil
1	tablespoon white wine vinegar
2	teaspoons Dijon-style mustard
¼	teaspoon pepper

◆ **Tear** off a 36x18-inch piece of heavy foil. Fold in half to make a double thickness of foil that measures 18x18 inches.

◆ **Combine** sliced potatoes, unpeeled garlic cloves, 1 tablespoon olive oil, and salt in a large mixing bowl; toss gently. Place potato mixture in the center of the foil. Bring up 2 opposite edges of the foil; seal with a double fold. Then fold in remaining ends to completely enclose the potatoes, leaving space for steam to build.

◆ **Grill** foil packet on the rack of an uncovered grill directly over *medium* heat for 35 minutes or until potatoes are tender, turning packet over occasionally. Remove garlic cloves and set aside to cool for 5 to 10 minutes. Close packet to keep potatoes warm.

◆ **Meanwhile,** in a screw-top jar combine chives, 1 tablespoon olive or cooking oil, vinegar, mustard, and pepper. Squeeze the paste from the grilled garlic cloves into the screw-top jar. Cover; shake well. If necessary, mash garlic with a fork. Transfer potato mixture to a large serving bowl. Pour garlic mixture over potatoes; toss gently to coat. Makes 6 side-dish servings.

NUTRITION FACTS PER SERVING: 317 cal., 6 g pro., 60 g carbo., 8 g fat, 0 mg chol., 5 g dietary fiber, 233 mg sodium.

GRILLED PIZZA

Forget carry-out tonight! Create crispy-crust pizza with your favorite toppings right outdoors on your grill.

PREPARATION TIME: 20 MINUTES • GRILLING TIME: 15 MINUTES

      Assorted toppings such as thinly sliced zucchini or yellow summer squash, broccoli flowerets, pepperoni slices, cooked and peeled shrimp, and/or sliced small tomatoes
1   10-ounce package refrigerated pizza dough
¾ cup pizza sauce or ⅓ cup purchased pesto
1½ cups shredded mozzarella cheese (6 ounces)

◆ **For toppings,** if using zucchini, summer squash, or broccoli, blanch vegetables for 2 minutes in enough boiling water to cover; drain and rinse immediately in cold water.

◆ **With your fingers,** pat the pizza dough into a greased 12-inch pizza pan or 2 greased 8x1½-inch or 9x1½-inch round baking pans. Place pan(s) on the grill rack directly over *medium* coals. Cover and grill for 5 minutes. Carefully remove the pan(s) from the grill.

◆ **Spread** pizza sauce or pesto onto the grilled crust. Sprinkle with desired toppings; top with shredded cheese. Return pizza to the grill rack. Cover and grill about 10 minutes or until pizza is heated through and cheese is melted, checking occasionally to make sure the crust doesn't overbrown. Makes 6 main-dish servings.

NUTRITION FACTS PER SERVING: 251 cal., 16 g pro., 26 g carbo., 9 g fat, 47 mg chol., 0 g dietary fiber, 653 mg sodium.

EASY APPETIZER PIZZAS

Prepare Grilled Pizza as directed above, *except* cut the roll of refrigerator dough into quarters. Flatten each quarter into a 5½- to 6-inch circle. Place circles on lightly greased pieces of heavy foil and continue as directed above. Cut each pizza into quarters. Makes 16 appetizer servings.

SUMMER SQUASH CASSEROLE

This creamy, herb-seasoned recipe is perfect for the garden's bumper crop of colorful summer squash.

PREPARATION TIME: 30 MINUTES • GRILLING TIME: 20 MINUTES

2	pounds yellow summer squash and/or zucchini
¼	cup chopped onion
1	10¾-ounce can condensed cream of chicken soup
1	8-ounce carton dairy sour cream
2	medium carrots, shredded (about 1 cup)
½	of an 8-ounce package (2 cups) herb-seasoned stuffing mix
¼	cup margarine or butter, melted

◆ **Slice** yellow squash and/or zucchini in half lengthwise. Then cut halves into ½-inch-thick slices (about 7 cups). Cook the yellow squash and/or zucchini and onion, covered, in a small amount of boiling water about 3 minutes or until crisp-tender. Drain well.

◆ **Stir** together soup, sour cream, and carrots in an extra-large mixing bowl. Stir in squash and onion; set aside.

◆ **Toss** the stuffing mix with the melted margarine or butter in a medium mixing bowl.

◆ **Tear** off two 24x18-inch pieces of heavy foil. Make a double thickness of foil that measures 24x18 inches. Arrange *half* of the bread mixture onto the foil in a 12x7-inch rectangle. Spoon vegetable mixture over bread mixture on foil. Top with remaining bread mixture. Bring up 2 opposite edges of foil; seal with a double fold. Then fold in remaining ends to completely enclose the mixture, leaving space for steam to build.

◆ **Grill** foil packet on the rack of an uncovered grill directly over *medium* to *medium-hot* coals about 20 minutes or until heated through. Makes 8 side-dish servings.

NUTRITION FACTS PER SERVING: 237 cal., 5 g pro., 23 g carbo., 15 g fat, 16 mg chol., 3 g dietary fiber, 562 mg sodium.

Potluck Favorites

When the occasion calls for a "dish to pass," turn to these potluck favorites—they'll not only feed a crowd, they'll stand out in a crowd, too. These side-dish and dessert specialties cut down on time in the kitchen, take advantage of summer's best produce, and are easy to tote to your next picnic.

Tortilla-Black Bean Casserole
(see recipe, *page 84*)

TORTILLA-BLACK BEAN CASSEROLE

The terrific taco taste in this easy-to-serve casserole will bring picnic-goers back for seconds. Pictured on pages 82-83.

PREPARATION TIME: 35 MINUTES • BAKING TIME: 30 TO 35 MINUTES

2	cups chopped onion
1½	cups chopped green pepper
1	14½-ounce can tomatoes, cut up
¾	cup picante sauce
2	cloves garlic, minced
2	teaspoons ground cumin
2	15-ounce cans black beans or red kidney beans, drained
12	6-inch corn tortillas
2	cups shredded low-fat Monterey Jack cheese (8 ounces)
2	medium tomatoes, sliced (optional)
2	cups shredded lettuce (optional)
	Sliced green onion (optional)
	Sliced pitted ripe olives (optional)
½	cup reduced-calorie dairy sour cream or plain yogurt (optional)

◆ **Combine** onion, green pepper, *undrained* tomatoes, picante sauce, garlic, and cumin in a large skillet. Bring to boiling; reduce heat. Simmer, uncovered, for 10 minutes. Stir in beans.

◆ **Spread** *one-third* of the bean mixture over bottom of a 3-quart rectangular baking dish. Top with *half* of the tortillas, overlapping as necessary, and *half* of the cheese. Add another *one-third* of the bean mixture, then remaining tortillas and bean mixture. Cover; bake in a 350° oven for 30 to 35 minutes or until heated through. Sprinkle with remaining cheese. Let stand for 10 minutes. Top with tomato slices, lettuce, green onion, and olives, if desired. Cut into squares. Serve with sour cream or yogurt, if desired. Makes 10 to 12 side-dish servings.

NUTRITION FACTS PER SERVING: 232 cal., 16 g pro., 35 g carbo., 6 g fat, 14 mg chol., 7 g dietary fiber, 586 mg sodium.

KEEPING WARM

To keep a casserole hot for an outdoor gathering away from home, wrap the well-heated casserole in foil or a heavy towel and stow in an insulated container. The temperature should stay above 140° for the food to be safe to eat.

GINGER-PEANUT PASTA SALAD

Toss corkscrew macaroni and crunchy vegetables with a zippy ginger dressing. To make a main-dish salad, add cooked shrimp or chicken strips.

PREPARATION TIME: 30 MINUTES • CHILLING TIME: 2 TO 8 HOURS

8	ounces corkscrew macaroni or fine noodles, broken up
20	fresh pea pods, tips and strings removed (about 1 cup)
1	medium kohlrabi, peeled and cut up, or 1 small cucumber, quartered lengthwise and sliced
2	medium carrots, cut into long thin strips (about 1 cup)
1	medium yellow and/or green sweet pepper, cut into thin strips
¾	cup thinly sliced radishes
½	cup bias-sliced green onions
3	tablespoons snipped fresh cilantro or parsley
	Ginger Salad Dressing (see recipe, *below*)
⅓	cup chopped peanuts

◆ **Cook** the macaroni according to package directions. During the last 30 seconds of cooking time, add the pea pods. Drain pasta and pea pods. Rinse with cold water and drain thoroughly.

◆ **Combine** macaroni and pea pods, kohlrabi or cucumber, carrots, sweet pepper, radishes, green onions, and cilantro or parsley in a large serving bowl. Add the Ginger Salad Dressing and toss gently to coat. Cover and chill for 2 to 8 hours.

◆ **To serve,** toss the salad again and sprinkle with peanuts. Makes 12 side-dish servings.

◆ **Ginger Salad Dressing:** Combine ¼ cup *salad oil,* 3 tablespoons *rice vinegar,* 2 tablespoons *sugar,* 2 tablespoons *soy sauce,* 1 teaspoon grated *gingerroot,* and 1 teaspoon *chili oil* or several dashes bottled *hot pepper sauce* in a screw-top jar. Cover and shake to combine. If desired, chill for up to 3 days. Shake before using.

NUTRITION FACTS PER SERVING: 165 cal., 4 g pro., 21 g carbo., 7 g fat, 0 mg chol., 1 g dietary fiber, 197 mg sodium.

GREEK TORTELLINI SALAD

Toss tortellini pasta and vegetables with the flavors of Greece—fresh lemon, fragrant mint, and tangy feta cheese.

PREPARATION TIME: 30 MINUTES • CHILLING TIME: 4 TO 24 HOURS

  2 9-ounce packages plain or tricolored refrigerated cheese-filled tortellini, cooked and drained
  2 red and/or green sweet peppers, cut into thin strips (2 cups)
  1 small red onion, thinly sliced
¼ cup sliced pitted ripe olives
½ cup rice wine vinegar or white vinegar
½ cup olive oil or salad oil
  3 tablespoons snipped fresh mint or 1 tablespoon dried mint, crushed
  3 tablespoons lemon juice
  2 tablespoons dry sherry
1½ teaspoons seasoned salt
  1 teaspoon garlic powder
⅛ to ¼ teaspoon crushed red pepper
½ cup crumbled feta cheese

◆ **Combine** cooked pasta, peppers, onion, and olives in a large bowl. For dressing, combine vinegar, oil, mint, lemon juice, sherry, seasoned salt, garlic powder, red pepper, and 1 teaspoon *ground black pepper* in a small bowl. Pour over salad; toss to coat. Cover; chill for 4 to 24 hours. Stir in cheese. Use a slotted spoon to serve. Makes 12 to 14 side-dish servings.

NUTRITION FACTS PER SERVING: 247 cal., 9 g pro., 23 g carbo., 14 g fat, 36 mg chol., 0 g dietary fiber, 484 mg sodium.

PICNIC POINTER

At outdoor gatherings, urge everyone to bring along a hearty appetite to eliminate leftovers. Don't carry home leftovers—discard them. Any food that has been exposed to warm temperatures can be harmful, even though it may still look appetizing.

SUMMER SLAW

Double this recipe and tote to the next neighborhood potluck.

PREPARATION TIME: 20 MINUTES • CHILLING TIME: 1 TO 24 HOURS

  6 cups preshredded coleslaw mix
  1 small red sweet pepper, seeded and coarsely chopped, or 1 medium orange, peeled,
      seeded, sliced, and quartered
 ½ of a jicama, peeled and cut into thin strips (1½ cups)
 ⅔ cup creamy cucumber, creamy Italian, buttermilk ranch salad dressing, or coleslaw dressing
 ⅓ cup toasted pecan pieces

◆ **Combine** coleslaw mix, pepper or orange, and jicama in a large mixing bowl.

◆ **Pour** dressing over coleslaw mixture and toss to coat. Cover and chill for 1 to 24 hours. Sprinkle with pecans before serving. Makes 6 side-dish servings.

NUTRITION FACTS PER SERVING: 207 cal., 2 g pro., 11 g carbo., 19 g fat, 1 mg chol., 4 g dietary fiber, 327 mg sodium.

TOASTING NUTS

To toast just a few nuts, place them in a small skillet. Cook over medium heat, stirring often, for 5 to 7 minutes, or until golden. Toast larger amounts in a shallow baking pan in a 350° oven for 5 to 10 minutes, stirring once or twice.

POTLUCK PASTA SALAD

Bottled Italian dressing adds zip to this vegetable and pasta combo.

PREPARATION TIME: 35 MINUTES • CHILLING TIME: 2 TO 24 HOURS

 4 ounces wagon wheel macaroni or desired pasta (1⅓ cups)
 4 ounces tricolored corkscrew macaroni or desired pasta
 1 teaspoon crushed red pepper
 1 medium red sweet pepper, cut into thin strips
 1 medium yellow squash and/or zucchini, halved lengthwise and sliced
 1 10-ounce package frozen peas, thawed, or 1½ cups shelled, cooked, and cooled fresh peas
 1 6-ounce can pitted ripe olives, drained
 4 ounces smoked cheddar cheese, cubed
 1 cup unblanched whole almonds, toasted (see toasting tip, *page 87*)
 ½ cup sliced green onions
 2 tablespoons snipped fresh tarragon, oregano, basil, or dill
 1 8-ounce bottle regular or nonfat Italian salad dressing

◆ **Cook** pasta according to package directions *except* add crushed red pepper to the cooking water. Rinse with cool water and drain thoroughly. Cool pasta to room temperature.

◆ **Combine** pasta, red sweet pepper, yellow squash or zucchini, peas, olives, cheese, almonds, green onions, and herb in a large mixing bowl.

◆ **Add** dressing to pasta mixture. Toss gently to mix. Cover and chill for 2 to 24 hours. Makes 12 side-dish servings.

NUTRITION FACTS PER SERVING: 302 cal., 9 g pro., 24 g carbo., 20 g fat, 10 mg chol., 3 g dietary fiber, 293 mg sodium.

KEEPING COOL

For your next picnic, use these tips for keeping cold foods cold when the weather is warm:
 ◆ Chill your cooler by filling it with ice for at least 30 minutes before packing it.
 ◆ Thoroughly chill foods before putting them in the cooler.
 ◆ In addition to ice or ice packs, pack some frozen foods, such as cans of juice concentrate, to thaw along the way and to help keep other foods cold.
 ◆ Wait until just before leaving home to pack your cooler.
 ◆ Avoid dry ice because it causes freezer burn on both food and bare skin.

DOUBLE PEANUT COOKIE BARS

No mixing bowl needed! Assemble the ingredients right in the pan for a fuss-free dessert that serves 36.

PREPARATION TIME: 10 MINUTES • BAKING TIME: 25 MINUTES • CHILLING TIME: 1 HOUR

- ½ cup margarine or butter
- 1½ cups graham cracker crumbs
- 1 14-ounce can *sweetened condensed* milk
- 1 12-ounce package peanut-butter-flavored pieces
- 1 6-ounce package semisweet chocolate pieces
- 1 cup chopped Spanish peanuts

◆ **Preheat** oven to 350°. Melt margarine or butter in a 13x9x2-inch baking pan in the hot oven. Remove from oven.

◆ **Stir** in crumbs; spread evenly in bottom of pan. Pour sweetened condensed milk evenly over crumbs. Sprinkle with a layer of peanut-butter-flavored pieces, a layer of chocolate pieces, and then the peanuts; press peanuts gently into mixture.

◆ **Bake** 25 minutes or until edges are golden brown. Chill at least 1 hour before cutting bars. Makes 36 bars.

NUTRITION FACTS PER BAR: 180 cal., 4 g pro., 17 g carbo., 11 g fat, 4 mg chol., 1 g dietary fiber, 112 mg sodium.

POTLUCK TIP

Transport cut bars in the baking pan, covered. To keep chocolate from melting, place in a cooler with ice until serving.

SUMMERTIME FRUIT TRIFLE

Purchased ladyfingers add convenience to this classic English dessert.

PREPARATION TIME: 45 MINUTES • CHILLING TIME: 3 HOURS

  2 cups fresh or frozen peeled peach slices or nectarines
  ½ cup fresh or frozen blueberries
  ⅓ cup sugar
  ¼ cup all-purpose flour
1½ cups skim milk
  ¼ cup frozen egg product, thawed, or 1 beaten egg
  1 tablespoon margarine
  1 teaspoon finely shredded orange peel
  ½ cup orange juice
  1 3-ounce package ladyfingers, split
  2 tablespoons cream sherry or orange juice
  2 cups sliced strawberries
  1 cup reduced-fat frozen whipped dessert topping, thawed
     Sliced strawberries (optional)
     Blueberries (optional)
     Fresh mint sprigs (optional)

◆ **Thaw** peaches and blueberries, if frozen.

◆ **For custard sauce,** combine sugar and flour in a heavy medium saucepan. Stir in skim milk and egg product. Cook and stir over medium heat until mixture is thickened and bubbly. Cook and stir for 1 minute more. Remove from heat. Stir in margarine, orange peel, and the ½ cup orange juice. Cool thoroughly, covered.

◆ **To assemble trifle,** cut ladyfingers in half crosswise. Arrange *half* of ladyfingers in a 2-quart glass bowl. Sprinkle ladyfingers with *1 tablespoon* of the sherry or orange juice. Top with *half* of the peaches, *1 cup* of the strawberries, and ¼ *cup* of the blueberries. Pour *half* of custard over fruit. Repeat layers. Pipe or spread dessert topping on top. Cover and chill at least 3 hours or until serving time. Garnish with additional strawberries, blueberries, and mint sprigs, if desired. Makes 8 to10 servings.

NUTRITION FACTS PER SERVING: 190 cal., 4 g pro., 34 g carbo., 4 g fat, 20 mg chol., 2 g dietary fiber, 128 mg sodium.

Guide for Grilling Success

Get your grilling off to a good start by choosing reliable equipment and utensils. Here are some hints to help you barbecue like a pro anywhere—from your own backyard to your favorite campsite.

Selecting a Grill

Grills come in many styles and sizes. Before purchasing a grill, consider the type of food you're cooking and time of year, as well as the size of group you're grilling for. Here are a few common types of grills:

Braziers

These simple and inexpensive shallow fireboxes fitted with adjustable grill grates are the most common type of grill. Designed for direct-heat cooking relatively close to the coals, braziers are perfect for cooking steaks, burgers, and chops. More upscale units have hoods, rotisseries, and air vents. All versions have grill grates that can be raised and lowered during cooking.

Portables

These lightweight miniature grills go anywhere—from apartment balconies, to the beach, to tailgate picnics. From open-style hibachis to small-scale covered kettles, portable grills are designed for direct-heat cooking methods. Small foods, such as hot dogs, burgers, steaks, kabobs, and chicken pieces, are well suited to these varieties.

Covered Grills

Kettle-shaped, rectangular, and square grills are all designed for closed-hood grilling. The deeper firebox allows for indirect cooking of larger cuts of meat. Air vents on the lid and base help control ventilation. Many have optional accessories, such as shelves that attach to the sides of the grill, and hooks to hold utensils within easy reach. Covered grills can also be used for direct-heat grilling.

Water Smokers

Perfect for long, slow cooking, these special covered grills have a water pan between food and fire. Dampened wood chunks sprinkled on the fire cook food continuously with steamy clouds of aromatic smoke for a penetrating barbecue flavor. Remove the water pan and lid to convert the smoker into an open brazier-style grill.

Gas Grills

Gaining in popularity is the fast-starting, easy-cleaning gas grill. Fueled by refillable propane tanks or by natural gas, the cooking temperature is easily controlled by adjusting the gas flame. Ceramic briquettes or lava rocks replace charcoal briquettes. Gas grills offer year-round cooking with direct heat, or covered grilling for roasting.

Tools of the Trade

The searing heat of a charcoal grill requires special utensils designed to protect the cook. Choose long-handled tongs, basting brushes, and spatulas, as well as heavy-duty oven mitts. And don't forget to wear a chef's apron to catch possible spatters and spills.

Skewers come in many lengths for holding small kabobs of meat and vegetables. If using bamboo or wooden skewers, soak in hot water for 30 minutes to prevent burning.

Stiff-bristled wire brushes whisk grill grids clean. Choose a long-handled brush, and using an oven mitt for protection, quickly scrape the grill while still hot for easy removal of baked-on food.

For grilling vegetables, try one of the ***enamel-coated grids*** designed to sit right on top of your grill. Small holes in these racks prevent bite-size pieces of food from falling through. Some models also have a raised edge allowing you to lift and turn foods in stir-fry fashion.

Hinged wire baskets are a good investment for cooking smaller cuts of meat, seafood, and vegetables. A long handle helps when turning frequently during cooking; a small clasp securely holds food in place. Brush basket lightly with oil to prevent foods from sticking.

An ***instant-read or rapid-response thermometer*** is essential for accurately judging doneness of meats. Clip right to your apron for easy access to perfect results every time.

Building the Fire

Charcoal Choices
Choose the fuel to fire up your grill:

◆ Traditional briquettes are the most common fuel for grilling. Their uniform pillow shape distributes heat evenly.

◆ Hardwood charcoal, including mesquite and hickory, burns hotter than briquettes.

◆ A mixture of briquettes and hardwood can be used to tone down the distinctive flavor of the hardwood charcoal. Try experimenting to find the flavor you prefer.

Flavor Options
Adventuresome cooks are experimenting with tossing hardwood chips or chunks onto a hot fire of traditional charcoal briquettes. You'll find mesquite and hickory chips and chunks, as well as alder, oak, and fruit woods such as apple, cherry, and peach. Read the package labels—chances are the chips will need to be soaked and drained before you use them, so they'll smoke, not flame.

Adding Herbs to the Fire

Water-soaked herb sprigs such as rosemary, thyme, oregano, and basil can be added directly to the hot coals. Also, try the new dried herb packets that resemble tea bags. These are custom-blended to enhance the flavor of meat, poultry, or fish.

How Many Briquettes?

For a medium-hot fire, spread coals in a single layer, barely touching each other, to extend about 2 inches beyond your food. For hotter fires, mound the coals closer together. For lower heat, spread the coals farther apart. Once you've determined the number of briquettes needed, push them into a mound for lighting.

Lighting the Fire

There are several methods for lighting a charcoal fire.

◆ **Liquid lighter fluid** is the most popular fire starter. Simply pour it over the briquettes and allow it to soak in (following manufacturer's directions), then ignite with a match.

◆ **Jelly and solid-cube starters** are premeasured, taking the guesswork out of how much fuel to use. Once lighted, they slowly burn, igniting the briquettes around them.

◆ **Chimney starters** are tall cylinders with a metal grate in the bottom for air circulation. To use, place crumbled newspaper or a solid-cube starter in the bottom of the chimney and stack briquettes on top, then ignite. When the coals are ready, carefully pour them out into the grill.

◆ Once lighted, standard briquettes take about 20 to 30 minutes to burn—coals should appear ash gray (in daylight) or glowing red all over (at night).

Safety First

◆ To reduce flare-ups, try raising the grill rack, covering the grill, arranging the coals with more space in between, or removing some of the coals.

◆ Keep a water bottle handy to mist the flames during cooking.

◆ Never use gasoline or alcohol as a substitute for lighter fluid. Also, never pour liquid lighter fluid onto burning coals.

◆ Keep young children well away from a hot grill.

◆ Place the grill on a level surface away from any combustible materials. If barbecuing on a deck, use a flame-resistant mat or pad underneath the grill.

◆ Never barbecue indoors on a gas or charcoal grill. Set the grill outdoors and make sure the area is well ventilated.

◆ Read the manufacturer's instruction manual before using a new gas or charcoal grill.

Get Set for Grilling

Arranging the Coals

Before you arrange the coals, you'll need to decide between direct and indirect cooking methods. Direct cooking means placing the food on the grill rack directly over the coals. For indirect cooking, coals will be arranged away from the food, so that juices from the food will not reach the coals, reducing flare-ups. To do this, use a disposable foil drip pan, or make your own by shaping heavy foil into a shallow pan shape that is large enough to cover the surface below the food. Place pan in the center of the firebox and mound the hot coals all around the pan with long tongs. Then, position the grill rack so additional coals can be added, if necessary.

For direct cooking, *top,* spread the hot coals evenly in a single layer. For indirect cooking, spread the hot coals around the perimeter of the firebox, surrounding a drip pan.

Testing Coal Temperature

Our recipes specify the hotness of the burning coals. Here is a surefire method for judging heat intensity: Carefully hold your hand, palm side down, where the food will be grilled. Count the number of seconds you can comfortably hold your hand in that position. Refer to the chart *below* to determine the coal temperature.

How Hot Is Hot?

Number of Seconds	Coal Temperature
2	hot
3	medium-hot
4	medium
5	medium-slow
6	slow

Note: For indirect cooking, you'll need *hot* coals to provide *medium-hot* heat over drip pan, *medium-hot* coals for *medium* heat, *medium* coals for *medium-slow* heat, and so forth.

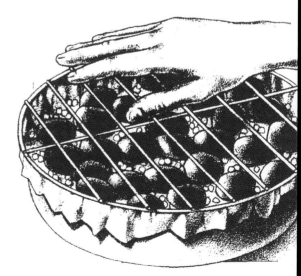

Nutritional Facts

So you can keep track of what you eat, each recipe in this book lists the nutritional values for one serving. Here's how we made our analyses. When a recipe gives a choice of ingredients (such as margarine or butter), we use the first choice in our analysis. Ingredients listed as optional were omitted from our calculations. Finally, all values were rounded to the nearest whole number.